PROCEEDINGS

of

THE LARC INSTITUTE

on

AUTOMATED SERIALS SYSTEMS

Held May 24-25, 1973
at the
Chase Park Plaza
St. Louis, Missouri

Coordinated By
Dr. Estelle Brodman, Librarian
Washington University School of Medicine
St. Louis, Mo.

Edited By
H. William Axford

Printed in the U.S.A.
Copyright © 1973 — The LARC Association
P.O. Box 27235
Tempe, Arizona 85282
Hardbound — ISBN 0-88257 — 097-8
Paperback — ISBN 0-88257 — 098-6

PREFACE

LARC INSTITUTE ON AUTOMATED SERIALS SYSTEMS
May 24-25, 1973
St. Louis, Mo.

All inventions go through a series of stages. There is a natural progression over time in the ability to employ an invention; going from scientist to engineer to technician to ordinary user, as the need to understand the scientific principles inherent in the invention and the difficulty of operating it lessen. A perfect example is the camera, which finally got to the point where the Kodak Company could advertise, "You press the button and we do the rest." The automobile is another instance of the simplification of a machine for use by the scientifically unsophisticated.

Computers, especially computers in library work, have already gone through the first three stages of the continuum, and are now being developed in a way that will allow the ordinary user to employ them without any concern for the manner in which they perform their duties. The so-called mini-computers and the ubiquitous laboratory computers fall in this class. It is therefore logical for a group of librarians to come together to discuss the library use of computers without concerning themselves about the "innards" of the machine. It is likely that many more such meetings will be held in the future.

On the other hand, part of the pleasure of working with a new invention—one still in the scientist and/or technician mode—is that standardization has usually not progressed to the point where individuality cannot be allowed to enter the picture. A glance at the many library computer systems which have been developed in the 1960's and then were allowed to disappear as other systems sprang into being with different individualities shows the action of this principle.

When we examine the history of computer librarianship, we see still another facet of the development of scientific inventions; that is, the necessity at one stage for using an external system, rather than developing one for oneself. When the users of an invention do not readily understand what makes it work or how it can be modified, they must depend upon an outside group who does know these things to set up the system and keep it in operating condition. It is this principle which has led to the multiplication of automobile service stations throughout the country, and it is the same principle which has made necessary the networking idea in computer librarianship, with the central node of the network taking on the problems connected with the computer itself. This is the reason that the Ohio College Library Center has been such a success—the time is right for its product.

Such a situation has many advantages, not the least of which is that it allows those with lesser knowledge and more routine attitudes to be successful in accomplishing the work which needs to be done. For those of us, however, who have enjoyed the intellectual challenge of a new and untried instrument, where the limits of possibility might be defined more by imagination than abundant funds, part of the fun of working with computers has undoubtedly been lost. It is to be hoped, if not expected, that librarians will all now go on to examine some other problem of librarianship with the same interest, freshness of vision, and imagination that the pioneers brought to computer librarianship in the decade and a half that has passed. Only in this way can we attract the best minds to our field.

> Estelle Brodman, Ph.D.
> Librarian and Professor of Medical History
> Washington University School of Medicine Library
> St. Louis, Missouri

CONTENTS

	Page
State of the Art Review Glyn T. Evans	7
The National Serials Data Program Paul Vassallo	15
Management Problems of the Network Manager Jacqueline Felter	25
Serline: On-Line Serials Bibliographic and Locator System Cecile C. Quintal	31
The Problems of Entering a Computerized Serials Network; or The Validity of Murphy's Law Priscilla Mayden	43
The PHILSOM Network; The Coordinator's Viewpoint Virginia Feagler	51
The PHILSOM Network; A Programmer/Analyst's View Neil Falvey	59
The PHILSOM Network; Maintenance and Design Millard Johnson	65
The PHILSOM Network; A User Library Viewpoint Dean Schmidt	71
Case Study of the Computer Assisted Serials System at the University of California, San Diego Don Bosseau	77
List of Institute Participants	121
The Institute Faculty	125

STATE OF THE ART REVIEW

Glyn T. Evans

Serials control has long been regarded as a prime target in the attempt to subject the internal processes of libraries to automated control. As an activity, serials control contains those characteristics which provide a pay-off when automated — that is, volatile records and files, the need for immediacy of information, the requirement for multiple access points, the decrease in human productivity as manual files increase in size and number, and so on.

For more than a decade systems have been operational in which, with varying degrees of success, the serials control function has been automated. I don't intend a detailed review in this paper, for three reasons.

Firstly, you will hear, in subsequent presentations, detailed descriptions of operational systems which embody many of the functions of serials control. Secondly, reports published in the last three years already provide excellent reviews. For example, there are reviews by Don Bosseau in *Advances in Librarianship*[1] and Don Hassmen in 'Serial Publications in Large Libraries'[2] Elizabeth Pan performed a Literature Review and Bibliography of Library Serials Control Systems[3] for the Five Associated University Libraries (FAUL), which was subsequently published through ERIC, and there is an excellent IBM Report 'Library Automation — Computerized Serials Control'[4]. Thirdly, no reports published subsequently, which I have seen at any rate, significantly change the situation reported in the above papers, although work cited in those papers has been fully explained.

Rather, I would like to examine some of the fundamental problems of automated serials control, and then speculate on the extent to which solutions can be found.

Library Control of Serials

The library has three modes in which it applies controls to serials. These are acquisition control, bibliographic description, and inventory control. These three are often blurred and overlaid, particularly in automated systems. One reason for this is that we have obscured the difference between the descriptive and the inventory functions of the serials catalog. Another is a failure to analyze fully the inventory aspect. I think it is necessary to re-establish these three entities.

a. The Bibliographic Record

The bibliographic record has to be clearly separated into those elements which are true of the serial whether or not the library has holdings, and those elements which pertain to local holdings and control. This separation is necessary for the full development of automated serials systems.

It is worth mentioning at this point the whole problem of serials cataloging. If any situation has been thoroughly confused in libraries, this is it. The full circle back to successive entry, the historical development of the codes, the reliance on example rather than principle within the codes, and more than anything else the inhibition of logical development by limitations in catalog production technique, have not helped serials control. An excellent discussion of these problems is presented by Kathryn Luther Henderson in 'Serial Publication in Large Libraries'[5].

Until these problems are finally resolved the full development of serials control systems will be severely delayed. It is possible that on-line access may hasten their solution.

The last major contribution to the theory of bibliographic control of serials was the publication of the Marc Serials Format, and Addendum No. 1 by the Library of Congress. The Format recognizes the varying practices which exist in libraries of differing types by allowing for tags for main entry (personal, corporate or conference) and title as it appears on the piece, abbreviated title, uniform title, full title, former titles and title variations, and, so help me, varying forms of the title. Implicit in this recognition is the acknowledgement that automated serials systems must account for such variation, particularly from the viewpoint of file access. The Marc format in general has separated out those elements which pertain to the individual library (except that it is impossible to see what Tag 265, subscription address, is doing there), and notes that holdings which are local, should be recorded in field Tag 850.

The other development which must be noted is the assignment of International Standard Serials Numbers (ISSN's). This is potentially of vital importance, or will be if publishers and their designers allow the number to appear on the piece. Perhaps even on the cover?

If we are well on the way to defining those elements which describe the piece, a great deal of work has to be done to define those additional data elements which must be used for the acquisition and inventory control functions. When I was at FAUL and worked on serials, we spent a considerable amount of time on this task. Indeed, a deal of work went into the definition of the definitions, and the definition of the attributes of serials data elements.

If effective serials control is to be achieved, the data must be thoroughly understood. If this isn't accomplished, any subsequent system will be collander-like and uncertain.

b. **The Acquisition Function**

The acquisition function comprises six related tasks; selection, order, order or subscription renewal, gifts and exchange, check-in, and claiming. Binding, holdings update and routing belong in the inventory function, that is to say, the handling of an item after it has been received in the library. One should note, however, that in many libraries, depending on their form of records and general system,

check-in and holdings are not updated until the item is bound. It is in this latter case that holdings update becomes an inventory control function.

At first glance, selection falls outside the realm of this paper; but is this necessarily so? I suggest that the information obtained from automated systems will affect selection.

The initial order for a serial seems to me to present no problem. Few libraries except those which are expanding rapidly, order new serials in such quantities as to justify a separate initial order system; but if the function can be built into a general in-process system, or as part of a total system, then so much the better. The critical requirement at this stage is the availability of good, authoritative serials catalog data, from which the library can build its record.

Subscription renewal is much more complicated, but since it occurs regularly, a well defined and executed routine should provide a return on the investment of time and money. Such a sub-system should monitor the allocation and expenditure of funds, changes in price, and provide warnings when subscriptions are not renewed. In addition, the module should interface with the claims system and the holdings file before payments are made. Gifts and exchange serials belong in this group in as much as they are alternative ways of acquiring serials. This mode of acquisition may be of minor concern to smaller libraries, but a larger library will need to account for this type of transaction.

This brings us to check-in, which alone has probably expended more energy and demanded more ingenuity than the rest of the automated serials control effort. The problem, of course, is that check-in demands an efficient interface between an item and its bibliographic description stored in the system. Difficult in a medium sized system with say 1500-2000 current serials, it becomes extraordinarily so for large libraries, collecting ten times or more that many. If one applies the rule of thumb that once a serials collection achieves a certain size the mix of frequencies of publication produces on the average 10 pieces per title per year, one is faced with checking in 15-20 thousand pieces for a medium sized library, and up to a half a million per year in a large research library. Dare I add, plus indexes?

These conditions have to be coupled with a performance standard which states that the contents of any packet should be passed against the system with confidence that the system will accept the data and automatically modify records, or reject the data and indicate why.

The efforts which have gone into serials check-in have aimed at facilitating this interchange between the open environment of the last batch from the mail room, and the closed environment of the system. The results of these efforts in general fall into two broad classes, which I call 'acceptance' and 'prediction', with a range of modes in between. 'Acceptance' techniques go some way to providing the check-in staff with at least an up-to-date guide or listing of current (i.e. expected) serials, but allow the operator to supply the final bibliographical details

with respect to volume, issue number, etc.

'Prediction' techniques attempt to provide the operator with an easy method of updating the files by printing on a list or by generating on a punched card the exact bibliographic data for the next expected issue. The Philsom system and the New York State Library system are two examples of the prediction system. They are different in that the New York system is constantly fine tuning itself as publishing patterns change. Between these two extremes of acceptance and prediction there are systems which do both.

Of course, no prediction system can completely service a library; there always has to be a system over-ride for the valid unexpected, receipt. It is fair to say that prediction techniques have been proven successful; that is, it is possible to predict the behavior of serials sufficiently accurately to make the exercise worth while.

The question is, which factors govern its success? One is the quality of the data and the programs. Another is the size of the library (I flinch at a tub file attempting to predict 20,000 serials). Yet another factor is the type of collection being built. If the collection is a core collection (or set of core collections) these standard serials will have regular publishing habits, and in general will come from North America or Western Europe where the communications are good. A comprehensive, research collection, on the other hand, will be larger and more diffuse, gathering publications from all over the world. As a consequence, more uncertainty creeps into the system. The decision as to which method to follow (or mix of methods) should be made on the above considerations, and not on the 'prediction' is better than 'acceptance' dictum or vice versa. There are two immediate hopes for solving the check-in problem. One is the International Standard Serial Number, with the proviso that it be accepted and used; the other is on-line technology. I will refer to these later.

At the very instant of check-in, when the holdings update is being performed, two other functions have to be addressed, one in acquisition control, the other in inventory control. The acquisition function is one part of the claim process; that is the claim for missing issues, if the piece is greater than the next successive issue in volume or part number. Even this simple routine poses a problem. Ponder, if you will, a weekly publication coming from Europe via surface mail. The pieces accumulate on the dock side waiting to be loaded, and they accumulate in a very logical way, first up — first on board. The ship arrives. One of the charming aspects of ships is that they are loaded from the bottom up; and unloaded from the top down. The last piece on is the first to be distributed in this country. It duly arrives at the library before its fellows which were published earlier and which were, of course, claimed by our super automated system. This is amusing, of course, and it doesn't happen very often; but it is worth citing as an example of problems stemming from the external environment, and may perhaps curb a search for a level of prediction perfection which is unattainable.

For completeness, one ought to mention the other part of claiming, that is the periodic review of the file to catch late issues on the basis of the last recorded check-in activity against any particular record, and the expected frequency of the item.

The Inventory Function

The inventory function comprises those actions which control the piece after it has been acquired. These are binding, (done sometimes on the basis of data gathered during check-in), holdings update (if this is a separate function from check-in), routing, and circulation control. I also will treat participation in a Union List of Serials as an inventory function.

Binding control can be a valuable by product of an automated serials system. Differing systems offer a variety of outputs from 'tickler steps' used for internal purposes, to binding forms that report pattern information for the use of the binder. A point to remember is that the binding title may not be the same as the full title. This can cause problems in data formatting if the function of the system is to carry pattern information since some punctuation may be necessary to break the title string into binding title lines. The MARC serials format does carry a tag to define title on the spine, but it is difficult to see what uitlity this has in a generalized sense since it will presumably vary from library to library, and who wants to know what LC's own spine title is?

At first glance, circulation control looks as if it does not belong in a serials control system, but the two systems do not exist in a vacuum. In fact, circulation is one part of the general inventory control problem, and data should automatically move to support the circulation junction from earlier efforts.

I merely want to ask one question, which is this. If one circulates serials, how does one reconcile the bibliographic holdings statement, which may be a very terse Volumes 1-100, 1874-1973, with the requirement to circulate, route, bind and rebind, at individual piece level, any section, or all sections, of Volumes 1-100, 1874-1973? Indeed, is such a reconciliation possible or does one start with two separate statements, the one a contraction of the other. Also, what effect does the binding function have on these requirements?

The union list of serials aspect is no more than a common inventory for a number of libraries. It may have bibliographic data (as defined earlier) in varying degrees of completeness, although it does not need a full bibliographic description for inventory purposes. In fact, sufficient data to identify the piece is all that is necessary provided holdings and libraries are identified. One aspect of a union serials list which has been sadly neglected is the need for cross references. With many libraries, all with individual practices, making possible multiple access points to the same record through the medium of cross references must be encouraged. Furthermore, the cross references absolutely must be fastened firmly to the master record and not allowed to float as dummy

records in the file, without control. If the latter is allowed to occur, blind cross references will appear, and the selection of subsets of the list become impossible since cross references are available only on an all or nothing basis.

I would like to refer back to the first of the three modules mentioned earilier, and talk about selection. Earlier, I noted that automation has a role to play in selection. At present, within the State University of New York, which comprises 72 campuses including 35 community colleges, we are planning a computer analysis of the union list of serials data base to determine the coverage of the serials collection by region, and by type of library within region. We hope that we can make some progress toward relationalizing the distribution of serial titles by eliminating unnecessary duplication, and by increasing the total number of titles held on a university-wide basis. The selection decisions can be assisted by the use of a machine data base. Coupled with a circulation and interlibrary loan system, we could really have a handle on serials.

The Optimal System

To finish this contribution, I would like to speculate I hope in a relatively informed way, on where serials control is going. It seems to me very clear that massive, on-line, serial control systems will emerge in the future. The work being done at OCLC on serials control, ranging from cataloging through check-in, binding and claiming is very encouraging, particularly since other regional groups are signing or negotiating agreements to participate with OCLC in joint service and development contracts.

What will these systems look like? First, they will carry serials catalog data. Through this data, the files will be accessed by search codes which will open all the forms of title fields, plus main entry and the other fields, including the ISSN, perhaps also CODEN. The local variants in bibliographic description must be accommodated in the file, and identified by each library.

When the file can be accessed readily, check-in can probably be performed through the CRT terminals. This will probably be as quick as pulling from a tub file; and certainly as quick as entering into a KARDEX. The file will be updated by keying in volume, issue number, etc.; or more likely, will display on the CRT screen the details of the next expected issue which can be accepted by typing a simple instruction code — with of course an over ride for the exceptions. Claiming and binding functions will be part of the system. The same system will fulfill the inventory functions, and will immediately be seen to be an on-line union list.

More important, serials control will be part of a total system which combines in process information, circulation, union lists, interlibrary loan and information retrieval in one package. I admit that all of this sounds like the depressingly familiar tale which has been told for years,

and is still no closer to realization. I suggest that there are some factors which have changed the game. First, there is the massive improvement in computer technology, which has dramatically lowered costs while increasing the speed of transactions. There is every reason to believe that this process will continue. Secondly, we anticipate that new technology will also reduce communications costs and that teleprocessing will become economically feasible in the near future.

Finally, the economic climate is fostering cooperation and joint effort at precisely the time when advances in technology, and increasing competence in bibliographic data handling hold promise of giving new meaning to cooperative endeavor.

What will it take to do the job? First, and of absolutely paramount importance, is the existance of a standard data base of authoritative serials cataloging data. This is vital. It is, frankly, a disgrace that such a base does not already exist, and I am delighted and relieved that Mr. Vassalo and his team are tackling this enormous project. The irony is that at precisely the time when we know how to do the job, and when the technology can help us, there is no data base from which to operate.

Secondly, I believe that the job should, and will, be done by bibliographic data centers, with all four of the above attributes (large computer, teleprocessing, expertise and motivation) and that libraries should become participants in such centers on a customer basis. In this way, the massive development costs can be shared, and the operational expenses shared among many libraries not carried individually.

I expect to see the kind of development, where as many as 300 terminals can access and work with the same data base simultaneously in an environment that is demonstrably cost beneficial for all participating libraries.

The corollary to this kind of approach, however, is that the days of local entrepreneurial programming efforts on the part of individual libraries will disappear. The fact of the matter is that it is becoming both too difficult and too expensive for an individual library.

In this paper I have tried to define and review what seems to be the salient points of serials control. If I may summarize, I would say that after much hard work, hard thought and hard investment over the years, the mechanical problems are becoming well understood, and that, granted the existence of a sound data base good on-line control systems will be available within the immediate future. The problem then will be those of massive implementation and acceptance.

And then the real problem can be faced. Having developed the tool, what will we do with it? How will it interface with other functions? Will we rationalize our collections, and improve our service?

Finally, a word from our sponsor, the user.

> 'I know, or think I know what a serial is when I come into the library with a citation from your information retrieval network, but then I run into trouble. You don't call it what I call it, and

you don't put it where I expect it to be. Sometimes you bind it when it is at its most useful, and sometimes you follow the barbaric practice of binding it without its index. Sometimes its late, sometimes its out of print, or just plain missing. Sometimes you haven't got it, and it takes a long time to get it.

But never mind; when I go to another library, they will call it something else again, and hide it somewhere different. At least I know that sometimes they will bind it without the index, like their neighbors!

Why don't you librarians get the computer to help you?'

Footnotes
1. Don L. Bosseau, "The Computer in Serial Processing Control," in *Advances In Librarianship* edited by Melvin J. Voight (Seminar Press, 1971).

2. Donald P. Hammer, "Serial Publications In Large Libraries: Machine Application," in *Serial Publications In Large Libraries* edited by Walter C. Allen (Urbana, Illinois; University of Illinois Graduate School of Library Science, 1970).

3. Pan, Elizabeth. *Library Serials Control Systems, A Literature Review and Bibliography* (Washington, D.C., ERIC Clearinghouse on Library and Information Sciences, 1970).

4. International Business Machines. *Library Automation: Computerized Serials Control* (New York, 1971).

5. Kathryn Luther Henderson, "Serial Cataloging Revisited," in *Serial Publications In Large Libraries, op. cit.*

THE NATIONAL SERIALS DATA PROGRAM

Paul Vassallo

In April 1972, the Library of Congress, the National Agricultural Library, and the National Library of Medicine announced the beginning of Phase III, the operational phase, of the National Serials Data Program.

This followed years of studies, discussions, task forces, committees, working papers, and projects. Many organizations contributed to the creation of this national program. While it is difficult to point to its genesis, certainly the active interest and concern of COSATI (the Committee on Scientific and Technical Information of the Federal Council for Science and Technology) played a catalytic role in causing the National Science Foundation to support a study by the Information Dynamics Corporation, summarized in the Creager and Sparks report *A Serials Data Program for Science and Technology* in 1965.[1] This report generated strong interest within the library community, with the National Science Foundation (NSF), the Association of Research Libraries (ARL), the Joint Committee on the Union List of Serials (JCULS), other various committees of the American Library Association (ALA), and the three national libraries—LC, NAL, NLM—contributing a tremendous amount of effort and ingenuity in bringing about Phase I or a National Serials Data Program in January 1968.

Phase I was supported by the three national libraries and administered by the Library of Congress, with the JCULS serving in an advisory capacity. It comprised various tasks. Task A was to compile a comprehensive set of data elements needed for the identification, description and location of serials. Task B was a user survey utilizing the data element list compiled in Task A; the survey, conducted by Nelson Associates, was inconclusive in some areas but did provide valuable data and some guidelines for establishing priorities. Task C produced the MARC Serials format. In the final report of Phase I, a pilot project was recommended to test some of the findings of Phase I.[2]

Phase II was the National Serials Pilot Project (NSPP), launched with a substantial grant from the National Agricultural Library and some additional support from LC, NLM, and the Council on Library Resources (CLR). The project was administered by ARL, with policy direction provided by the National Libraries Task Force (NLTF). The aim of the project was threefold: (1) to create a machine-readable file containing live serials from the science and technology holdings of the three national libraries; (2) to produce a number of preliminary listings, including a union list and other lists of interest to management; and (3) to write one or more reports presenting information on the universe of serials, discussing problems and solutions, and making recommendations. A serial was defined as "a publication in successive parts bearing

numerical or chronological designations and intended to be continued indefinitely." The final report of NSPP[3] concluded that "a national serials data program appears to be both technically and economically feasible . . ."

On the conclusion of the National Serials Pilot Project in June 1971, the National Libraries Task Force, which has provided policy direction to the NSPP, continued discussions to seek means for moving into the next phase. In March 1972, the Library of Congress, on behalf of the three national libraries, issued a *Summary of National Serials Data Program*[4] and in April 1972 announced the beginning of Phase III. The announcement stated that, with the joint support of the Library of Congress, the National Agricultural Library, and the National Library of Medicine, the National Serials Data Program would continue the development of a central machine-readable source of serial cataloging information and an economically feasible system of handling serials that would eliminate the costly duplicative input and conversion projects that would otherwise be necessary.

The stated intent of Phase III is to provide to the three national libraries—and to other research libraries as well—an authoritative automated bibliographic resource upon which serials processing systems can be built; a base record of serial titles to which the International Standard Serial Number can be permanently affixed, thus ending the confusion about precise identification of serials; a machine-readable bibliographic resource for serials that will supply important cataloging information to libraries and at the same time permit the uniform transfer of data on serials among libraries; a base from which several kinds of library tools can be developed; and, finally, a serial system that will constitute the U. S. segment of the developing International Serials Data System.

Organization

The Director of NSDP operates under policy guidelines determined by the Librarian of Congress, the Director of the National Agricultural Library, and the Director of the National Library of Medicine, and reports on administrative matters to the Deputy Librarian of Congress.

As the U. S. National Center (USNC) for assignment of the International Standard Serial Numbers (ISSN) for the international control of serial publications, the NSDP maintains liaison with the International Center of the International Serials System (IC/ISDS) in Paris, France.

A National Advisory Committee to the NSDP serves as a communications link with the varied user community to which the NSDP ultimately will respond. It focuses also on advising the director of the NSDP on the needs of the different clients who will benefit from this national program.

Progress in developing a system

The stated objective of the NSDP is to develop a national system of bibliographic control over all serial publications. In reaching that objective, the Program has developed certain priorities essentially reflective of the availability of funds. It was determined that the operational phase should develop on a systematic basis by tackling one task that could be managed and kept under control. The limited availability of funds also prescribed that the first task be limited. Thus the top priority was assigned to utilizing bibliographic data on serial titles from the three national libraries for establishing the initial NSDP data base. The current cataloging data was considered the best source for building the initial file. Plans were developed to write programs to utilize serials files that exist in machine-readable form from the three national libraries.

Developments at the level of the three national libraries were coincidental with developments of the ISSN as an international standard and the International Serials Data System as an international organization.

The International Standard Serial Number

In May 1968, the American National Standard Institute Committee on Standardization in the Field of Library Work Documentation and Related Publishing Practices (ANSI-Z.39 Committee) organized Subcommittee 20 charged with the "development of a standard registration code for periodical and serial publications." On November 25, 1970, ANSI approved the "Identification Number for Serial Publications" as a national standard and thereby created the Standard Serial Number (SSN). The Library of Congress had agreed to serve as the registration center subject to the availability of necessary funds, manpower, and space.

Concurrent with this American development were efforts at the international level through the International Organization for Standardization (ISO) TC46 Committee. At its meeting in Oslo, Norway, in June 1970 the ISO/TC46 Working Group I recommended an international review of the pending U. S. standard (SSN). Another development was the emergence of a joint UNESCO/International Council of Scientific Unions (ICSU) feasibility study on the establishment of a world science information system (UNISIST). UNISIST is an acronym that stands both for the feasibility study and for the recommended future programs to implement its recommendation.[5] ICSU also funded a study resulting in the *Report on the Feasibility of an International Serials Data System.*[6]

Thus, all these were simultaneous developments on both the national and international level, all focusing on systems development and the formulation of standards. Fortunately, the task ahead was so enormous that cooperation seemed advantageous to all parties concerned.

After several meetings, working group discussions, analyses and reactions, ISO/TC46 approved a draft international standard ISSN at its meeting in The Hague in early October 1972. This standard is currently being circulated among member organizations for ratifications. Thus, for all intents and purposes, the standard is being implemented as accepted.[7]

The International Standard Serial Number (ISSN) is an eight-digit code that is assigned to a unique title (key title) of a serial publication. The eight digits utilize Arabic numerals from 0 to 9 (with a minor exception, as noted below). In every ISSN, the last digit—while considered part of the number—is actually a computer-calculated check digit designed to guard against transcription errors. (For those familiar with check digits, it is calculated on a modulus 11 using weights 8-2 and appears as: ISSN 1234-5679; in the rare instance where a check digit value of 10 is calculated, the letter X is substituted to retain the 8-digit format.) The standard defines a serial as: "a publication, in print or in non-print form, issued in successive parts usually having numerical or chronological designations and intended to be continued indefinitely. Serials include periodicals, newspapers, annuals (reports, yearbooks, directories, etc.); the journals, memoirs, proceedings, transactions, etc. of societies; and monographic series."

The ISSN is assigned to a "key title", which is essentially "title as it appears on the piece", with some minor modifications. As the key title has to be unique, qualifiers are used to make duplicate titles unique. Thus information such as place or beginning date of publication is added to a title to distinguish it from another title already existing, as in the case, for instance, of *Medicina* and *Medicina* (Madrid). Rules for assignment of key title and the use of qualifiers are given in the *ISDS Guidelines*.[8] While the development of the ISSN as an international standard was the responsibility of ISO/TC46, the responsibility of implementing it rests with ISDS.

ISDS

Various individuals and institutions associated with the UNISIST developments, including ICSU, ANSI-Z.39, ISO/TC46, IFLA, and other international organizations concerned with bibliographic controls worked towards the development of the International Serials Data System within the concept of UNISIST. The French Government offered to support this system in cooperation with UNESCO, and an International Center of ISDS was established in Paris. The IC/ISDS, with headquarters in the Bibliotheque Nationale, Paris, is responsible for the administration of the assignment of ISSN to the national or regional centers. The IC also serves as the international registry for the ISSN and for the coordination of efforts of the national and regional centers to develop and maintain a uniform international system of control over serial publications. In addition to the United States, the United Kingdom and Australia have established national centers. The

Director General of UNESCO, in a letter of November 6, 1972, informed member states of the creation of ISDS and extended the invitation to participate by designating national centers to cooperate with this System. The designation of NSDP as the United States National Center was cited in the Director General's letter as an example of the cooperation desired.

As the United States National Center, the National Serials Data Program (NSDP) is the sole agency responsible for the control and assignment of ISSN in the United States. The concept has been established that a national center is authorized the use of ISSN from the IC solely for those publications emanating from the respective nation.

As a result of negotiations with the various participants involved in establishing the International Serials Data System, the R. R. Bowker Company was authorized to number with ISSN the approximately 60,000 titles in the Bowker Serials Bibliography, composed of Volumes I and II, entitled *Ulrich's International Periodicals Directory* and Volume III, entitled *Irregular Serials and Annuals: An International Directory*. The R. R. Bowker Company was also authorized to number the contents of a *Supplement* to the Bowker Serials Bibliography, published in December 1972. Negotiations between the NSDP and Bowker are being carried on to permit the numbering with ISSN of the *New Serial Titles* cumulation for 1950-70 scheduled for publication by Bowker in late 1973.

As the national center for the assignment of an ISSN and key title to each serial, the NSDP receives requests for assignment of ISSN. Standard bibliographic tools are used to verify data; data is checked against the NSDP file and Bowker file to avoid duplicate ISSN assignment. If an ISSN exists, NSDP informs the requesting institution; if no ISSN exists, one is assigned for American imprints or NSDP requests an ISSN from the International Center in Paris for foreign titles. NSDP then keyboards the necessary bibliographic data and the corporate authority and holdings data into the NSDP files, and creates and sends computer-produced products and publications to the three national libraries, the International Center, and the user community.

The NSDP Data Base

The NSDP data base consists of records of titles in machine-readable form augmented with aperture cards for each title in the file. Since the identification of certain data can only be ascertained by looking at the serial itself, and since this is a virtual impossibility because of the variety of resources for the data, it was determined that a surrogate of the issue itself is needed. Aperture cards showing the cover and/or title page and masthead serve to augment the information provided in the bibliographic data generated by the contributing institution. Once the record for the particular serial is developed, the key title and ISSN are punched on the aperture card for retention as a visual verification file,

which thereby serves as the final arbiter over the question of duplication of titles.

The NSDP record consists of those data elements that are identified in the ISSN as an international standard and are needed for input into the International Serials Data System (ISDS) by the national centers, plus additional data elements which we consider necessary for the national set. The listing below presents an adaptation of elements from the MARC Serials format considered as being needed for the unique identification of a serial. It must be understood that while the same tags are used for the selected data elements as in MARC, there are differences in interpretation. NSDP used the key title as the benchmark, whereas MARC Serials uses the full title as a benchmark. Thus linked titles such as variant title, former title, successor title, and related title, in NSDP refer to the key title whereas in MARC they refer to the full title. There are a few other minor adaptations which have been coordinated with the MARC Development Office in LC. The first nine elements are those considered essential and absolutely required of each center for input into ISDS, the first two being primarily for housekeeping purposes. Since the international set does not include an element for author (issuing body) and since we feel this is essential for American users, we have included it as a priority element in the record. Elements 11-26 comprise the rest of the elements in the international set as specified in the ISSN standard. Elements 27-33 are additional elements considered desirable for the national record. It is realized, of course, that many other data elements may be considered desirable by a variety of users. Some may be of national importance, others of local or limited need. The NSDP is providing the basic set of elements that can be amplified upon by local users if they feel there is a need.

Essential ISDS Data Elements	MARC Serials Fields
1 Date of Entry (or most recent amendment)	008
2 Centre Code	008
3 ISSN	022
4 Key Title	222
5 Variant Title	246
6 Start Date	008
7 Country of Publication	008
8 Alphabet of Original Title	008
9 Imprint	260

National Data Element

10 Author Entries	700
	710
	711

Other ISDS Data Elements

11	Coden*	030
12	Publication Status	008
13	Type of Publication	008
14	End Date	008
15	Frequency*	008/310
16	Language*	008/041
17	UDC, DC or LC**	080/082/050
18	Abbreviated Title***	210
19	Former Title(s)	780
20	Successor Title(s)	785
21	Other Language Edition of	759
22	Has Other Language Edition	769
23	Inset in or Supplement to	779
24	Has Inset or Supplement	789
25	Related Title	787
26	Coverage by Abstracting Services*	510

Additional National Data Elements

27	Date and Volume Designations	362
28	LC Card Number*	010
29	U.S. Supt. Doc. No.*	086
30	Title as it Appears on the Piece (when different from key title)	200
31	NLM Call No.*	060
32	NAL Call No.*	070
33	Notes	500

*To be supplied when readily available.
**UDC or DC are preferable. LC Classification may be provided if UDC or DC are not available.
***Journal title abbreviation as provided by the "International List of Periodical Title Word Abbreviations."
****Elements 19-25 should be represented by their respective ISSN (when available).

Building the initial file

In observing its existing priority as a program of the three national libraries, the NSDP determined that the best approach to the creation of an initial file would be to interface with each of the three libraries on their current cataloging of serials. Concerted efforts were made as soon as staff was available to work out and test procedures for absorbing the various inputs from each source. This involved the integration of NSDP procedures within the internal cataloging processes of each national library. By early February 1973, NSDP was receiving cataloging data and surrogates from each of the national libraries for editing, conversion, and inclusion in the NSDP data base. The annual intake is estimated at 10,000 titles from LC and approximately 2,000 titles each from NAL and NLM. This process also includes the production of

aperture cards for all titles added to the NSDP data base. The absorption of data from three sources, each reporting on its own internal forms and worksheets creates many problems. The NSDP, as a cooperative program of the national libraries, seeks to minimize differences through the development of a uniform reporting sheet. Another problem relates to transliteration schemes. The NSDP is committed to utilizing international standards where they exist. At present, there is an ISO standard for the romanization of the Cyrillic alphabet. The NSDP, therefore, is required to submit data on Cyrillic titles to ISDS in this form, while the form used by the three national libraries differs. Also, diacritics are required for input to ISDS. Not all three national libraries use diacritics in their cataloging.

With current cataloging information being utilized for the development of the initial data base, we have also performed some tasks to permit the incorporation of existing serial files in machine-readable form from the three national libraries. These consist of the National Library of Medicine/Union Catalog of Medical Periodicals (NLM/UCMP) file, the National Agricultural Library/Cataloging and Indexing (NAL/CAIN) file, and the National Serials Pilot Project (NSPP) file. Computer programs have been written to convert records from the NLM/UCMP file (20,000 titles) and the NAL/CAIN file (2,200 titles) to a MARC Serials type file. The NSPP file, consisting of records for 7,049 titles, was orginally created as a MARC Serials type file. Computer programs are being written that take the MARC versions of these three files and convert them as best as possible to the NSDP set, with certain factors having to be taken into consideration. The NAL, NLM, and NSPP data elements do not automatically map into NSDP elements. The NLM file is in all upper case. The next step is to merge all three files together, sort the merged file by title, with "diagnostic worksheets" printed for use by editors.

In addition to incorporating these serial files and current cataloging output from the three national libraries to develop the initial NSDP file, the program is also producing other files.

The NSDP Corporate Entry Authority File

In addition to the basic file of records on the serial titles, the NSDP is also establishing a Corporate Entry Authority File (according to the Anglo-American Code) which includes the entry used by NSDP for the issuing body and the entries for that body used by the three national libraries. Our study of the usages of the three national libraries reveals extensive differences. The Library of Congress has been using Anglo-American only since March 1967; consequently, there are many previously established entries that have not been changed. The NSDP Corporate Entry Authority File shows the NSDP entry as well as the LC, NAL, and NLM forms used for that particular issuing body.

The authority file, which is currently being built up from the current cataloging from the three libraries, is designed to serve the following purposes:

a. to document the form of name used by NSDP (constructed according to the Anglo-American Code);

b. to insure accuracy and uniformity in the use of any name added to the NSDP data base;

c. to record variant forms of authors' names, tracing the necessary cross references and indicating the sources used for this information;

d. to record the necessary history of reorganizations and changes of name for an author, tracing the appropriate cross references and citing the source for this information;

e. to record the form of name used by any of the three national libraries, when different from that chosen by NSDP;

f. to record the ISSN for those titles with which an author is associated.

Holdings Record

A third file in the NSDP is the holdings record, accessible by ISSN and key title. The reporting library is identified by the NUC code. Holdings are not given in detail but are categorized according to the report of the holding library. The categories in the holdings record are:

    Not received
    Completeness unknown
    Complete, or substantially complete
    Substantially incomplete (scattered issues)
    Held, limited time only
    Received but not retained

Service to the National User Community

The National Serials Data Program has assigned its top priority to providing a support service to the three national libraries that will create a data base on the serial publications they hold. Staff energies have been dedicated to that priority, and requests for staff on appropriated funds for the next fiscal year have been based on service to the three national libraries being the first priority.

The National Serials Data Program, however, is a national program. As such, it was designated as the United States National Center for the International Serials Data System. In order to fulfill this role the NSDP must, in addition to continuing to provide support to the three national libraries, develop mechanisms and provide a service to the national user community. Increasing evidence on the need for such a development has been received by the Program and the Library of Congress in the form of a number of resolutions and letters. In order to function within the International Serials Data System, the NSDP must also be responsive to all in the national user community. To ensure reciprocity,

it must also be responsive to requests from other national centers in ISDS. We stand to benefit from this cooperative effort.

The NSDP is currently funded with equal support from LC, NAL, and NLM, as well as a grant from the Council on Library Resources. Funding for fiscal year 1974 is to be on a 4:1:1 basis with the Library of Congress quadrupling its support through a direct Congressional appropriation and NAL and NLM maintaining the current level of support. The increased funding, however, will only provide for continuing the response to the three national libraries.

The Board of Directors of NSDP realize the program's responsibility as a national program and will be seeking additional funding for this purpose through a grant from an outside source.

With the combined support of a varied national user community, the National Serials Data Program is well on its way towards becoming a truly national program.

REFERENCES

1. Information Dynamics Corporation. *A Serials Data Program of Science and Technology.* Prepared by William A. Creager and David E. Sparks. Reading, Massachusetts: 1965.

2. U. S. Library of Congress. Information Systems Office. *National Serials Data Program: Phase I Final Report.* Washington, D. C.: 1969.

3. U. S. Library of Congress, *ibid.*

4. Association of Research Libraries. Johnson, Donald W. *Toward a National Serials Data Program: Final Report of the National Serials Pilot Project.* Appendix C, p. 41.

5. *UNISIST: Study Report on the Feasibility of a World Science Information System.* UNESCO. Paris, 1971.

6. UNISIST/ICSU-AB: Working Group on Bibliographic Descriptions. *Report on the Feasibility of an International Serials Data System, and Preliminary Systems Design.* Prepared by M. D. Martin and C. I. Barnes. London. April, 1970.

7. International Standard Serial Numbering (ISSN). September 1972.

8. *ISDS Guidelines.*

MANAGEMENT PROBLEMS OF THE NETWORK MANAGER

Jacqueline Felter

When I accepted Dr. Brodman's invitation to participate in this Institute I agreed to speak as the manager of a library serials network, but when I began collecting my thoughts for this assignment I asked myself "What *is* management?" "Who is participating?" and "are there really problems?"

Webster has a definition of management that is appropriate, I think: "management is the judicious use of means to accomplish an end."

The participants in a library serials network are using a common "judicious means" of organizing and keeping account of the serials publications they receive—housekeeping, if you will. This relationship may be a network, or lead to a network operation, but it may also be less structured; it may be simply several libraries for which a computer-assisted serials system is feasible if they work together but not possible for one alone. This institutions forming the group may set up jointly a central operating station, or, more likely, several libraries "may draw on the services of one for individual rather than common purposes."[1] In other words, one member of the group assumes responsibility as a service bureau.

The factors in the management of a joint or community enterprise may well be different, probably more complex, than in an individual undertaking. Whether or not they become problems depends on how they are handled. I hope today to suggest means of preventing the elements of management from becoming problems.

As I see them the factors are financial, human, and serial. The characteristics of serial publications have been often belabored, and since they affect alike single and multiple library systems, I shall pass over them. I prefer to speak about managing money and managing people.

First of all, budgeting for a serials network or cooperative must be adequate. It is not easy to draw up a realistic budget because there is still a paucity of cost data. Individual libraries heretofore have not had to analyze every task and apply a price tag. Even if they have done so, the same unit prices may be unrealistic for a common system.

When a library that has developed a system for internal use decides to make its service available to other libraries it can easily fall into a financial trap. One may say, "I am doing this job for myself anyway, so I shall charge my customers only enough to pay the out-of-pocket expense of the service." But the unit cost determined in this way seldom includes incidental expense such as telephone charges and postage or labor and building overhead. As a result the library that is functioning as a service bureau finds itself carrying an inordinate financial load. The service facilitator must *not* be expected to write off overhead costs.[2]

When a library becomes a service bureau, it would be much wiser to set up a separate operating unit for the joint enterprise; determine the expenses of the unit, including such easily overlooked items as overhead, fringe benefits for personnel, secretarial and accounting assistance, telephone, TWX, and postage costs, and budget accordingly; and then divide the cost by the number of participants, counting itself as one of them. Thus, the expense is evenly spread. Undoubtedly, if a number of libraries were to set up a new central service unit in which all cost elements would be identified, a budget would be made, and the expenses would be divided in this way.

Divided into equal parts, this would be good, if the participating libraries were of equal size and/or make equal demands on the service, or, as Sinclair put it in his recently published article in *Special Libraries*, if they operated at equal or similar rate of efficiency.[1] If the libraries vary in size, or if one component is much larger than the rest, however, how does one apportion the cost? Sinclair went on to suggest "an adaptation of marginal analysis to the schedule of charges determined by the facilitator. . . . Marginalism suggests that the charge at a given level of output should be determined by summing up a series of marginal costs . . ." If then, the cost is divided evenly among the participants, the large library, or the more efficient one, "achieves a higher volume of input at a lower average rate than [the smaller or] less efficient participant whose input volume was lower. It also suggests that in order to maintain the proportionality condition . . . a more efficient [or larger] participant should be charged more than the less efficient [or smaller] by the margin of efficiency at given levels of input to the facility."

Sinclair says rather elaborately that there should be a common denominator, or minimum base fee, for all participants, with additional unit fees, or graded fee levels, for those whose volume of input exceeds the minimum.

There is another financial booby trap to beware of—the grant, or, rather, the end of the grant. It is not unusual, particularly if the participating libraries are setting up a new processing center or a new system, to obtain a grant to cover the initial investment. It must be remembered, though, that grants rarely are renewed time and again forever, and the participants must be prepared to pick up the tab when the system is operational. It behooves the facilitator, also, to prepare an economical operating program and a budget that, as much as the crystal ball permits, takes into account the factor of inflation, and to advise the participants well in advance the amount of the share each must pay.

And that brings us to people. Anderson said that "library literature and records of professional meetings reveal more talk about library cooperation and less action than about any subject in librarydom."[2] And there appears to be general, if pessimistic, agreement among the talkers and writers that, as Uri Bloch put it, human barriers, not the absence of new technology, are impeding network development.[3]

For a network or cooperative service to be successful and for the participants to get full benefit all parties must be committed to it. The commitment must be in principle and extend to procedures and to the expenditure of local funds, or as the homely expression states it, to put their money where their mouth is. It would be wiser to stay out of a cooperative venture if the local priorities are likely to come into conflict with group priorities.

In the processing of serials records, one of those tasks in which bibliographical precision assumes great importance and may evoke sharp differences of opinion, commitment to procedure set up by someone else may be more difficult than commitment of funds. Minder acknowledges individualism as the first factor of cooperation[4], and Dougherty points out the fact that there is high correlation between the success of joint ventures and the degree of modification of local procedures they require. Nevertheless, it was Veaner's opinion that we must "realize that the computer is an instrument of standardization"[5] and Bloch characterized standardization, or rather refusal to accept standards, as "the major stumbling block to network development."[3] Few systems have been designed as skillfully as the shared cataloging system of OCLC especially with regard to the ability to satisfy most local idiosyncracies.

A large measure of standardization is the *sine qua non* of the cost-effective cooperative, computer-assisted serials system. Paulson said that "we need to examine our thinking about . . . the need for local variation from national practices[6]." Bloch states firmly that "once a standard has been accepted, it should be changed only for the most important reasons. To expect continuous adaptations to a system only because the standards committee [or service facilitator] cannot come to grips with all the problems at the beginning, is to invite certain disaster."[3] Dougherty agrees, adding that librarians often accept the concept of standardization, then undermine it with variations of details.[7] And, I agree with all of them.

I said I would talk about people, and have been talking about standards. But, I have not really gone off the subject. People determine and live with the standards. There has to be some accomodation. It is necessary, but sometimes not easy, to live with standards that do not match one's idea, or ideal, of perfection. Dougherty reminds us that "the quest for perfection can sabotage the foundation of the strongest cooperative,"[7] and Ake cautions that to be a purist can be outrageously expensive.[8] As Galvin says, "sharing . . . services is almost always going to prove second best to sole ownership,"[9] but, particularly when the service is better performed with the help of a computer, the benefits or results can be gained only through joint effort.

Probably all of us have related the foregoing comment on standardization to the bibliographic and holdings details of serials and serials records management. There are some other facets of the operation that do not penetrate so deeply the philosophical founda-

tions of library work. These are the operational details where conformity to an established procedure oils the wheels of the machine: schedule and deadlines, for instance. When a system is using batch mode no member has the right to hold up the whole operation if he cannot keep on schedule, and, if his input is late, he should not be surprised if the batch is processed without it. The importance of keeping on schedule may apply to an on-line operation, too; few of us enjoy the luxury of using a dedicated computer and allocation of shared time must, for reason of economy, be very tight.

Lest these words sound very severe, rest assured that I would eschew rigidity for its own sake. The best rule I know for successful management of a network or cooperative system is: evaluate each task of the operation and keep the weights in balance. Govern with standards and schedules and rules the tasks that are the most sensitive, those which must perform in harmony to create a smooth-running machine. To permit individual variations in tasks that are not so-called "moving parts" will make the network more useful and more attractive to the participants. I like Minder's summing up of the factors in a successful cooperative operation[4]:

    individualism — the right to some personal gain from the venture
    altruism — the willingness to relinquish personal gain for the benefits to other participants
    group welfare — the benefits gained through joint effort
    well defined authority — acceptance of management.

REFERENCES

1. M. P. Sinclair, "A Typology of Library Cooperatives", *Special Libraries*, 64:181-186, April 1973.

2. J. F. Anderson, "In the National Interest", *Library Journal*, 97:1774, May 15, 1972.

3. Uri Bloch, "Is It Technology that Impedes Network Development?", *Library Journal*, 98:136-137, January 15, 1973.

4. T. L. Minder, "Organizational Problems in Library Cooperation", *Library Journal*, 95:3448-3450, October 15, 1970.

5. A. Veaner, "The Application of Computers to Library Technical Processing", *College and Research Libraries*, 31:36-42, January, 1970.

6. P. J. Paulson, "Networks, Automation, and Technical Services; Experience and Experiment in New York State", *Library Resources and Technical Services*, 13:516-519, Fall 1969.

7. R. M. Dougherty, "The Praradoxes of Library Cooperation", *Library Journal*, 96:1767-1770, May 15, 1972.

8. R. S. Ake, "Reimburse for Differences", *Library Journal*, 97:1775, May 15, 1972.

9. T. J. Galvin, "Not in Our Stars, But In Ourselves", *Library Journal*, 97:1772, May 15, 1972.

SERLINE: ON-LINE SERIALS BIBLIOGRAPHIC AND LOCATOR RETRIEVAL SYSTEM

Cecile C. Quintal

As an aid to the handling of the interlibrary loan traffic throughout the National Library of Medicine's Regional Medical Library Network, a cooperative activity was undertaken on the national level to produce a national index of substantive biomedical serials. The goal of this project was to produce an on-line finding tool of ca 6500 biomedical titles by region and by library speedily and inexpensively.[4] The data base would have bibliographic information as well as location data. It would be restricted to those titles for which there has been or are likely to be significant document demands. A practical method of measuring this demand is the inclusion of a title in one or more of the major biomedical abstracting and indexing publications.

In 1972, the National Library of Medicine requested that the Medical Library Center of New York acquire the existing regional union lists in the *Union Catalog of Medical Periodicals* (UCMP) format for merging to form the basis of the Serline (serials on-line) Data Base. For regions which had been unable to produce a UCMP-compatible list a complete title checking list of the titles to be included in the file was supplied to capture data on titles owned by the Regional Medical Library and resource libraries. Maintaining up-to-date holdings data for 117 libraries is an extremely costly operation. However, if this data were replaced by a locator code to the holding library (with the understanding that a library would not list itself as holding a title unless a near complete run was held), an inexpensive locator tool could be produced and maintained at a reasonable cost.

Serline was developed as an on-line retrieval system, its goal being the provision of direct and immediate access to stored bibliographic and locator data for serials held by libraries in the Regional Medical Library Network.

DESCRIPTION OF THE SYSTEM

Serline operates under program called ELHILL. This is the same software package which drives the Library's Medline (Medlars On-Line) retrieval system. The communications network operated by Tymshare, Inc. gives telephone access in about forty-five cities to the Serline data base on NLM's IBM 370/155 computer. Access is achieved through teletype, TWX, IBM 2741's, and other types of terminals operating at 10, 15, or 30 characters per second. Eleven Regional Medical Libraries will coordinate the Serline service in their regions.

Search formulations are entered without any punctuation or secondary keying requirements. All other instructions to the program are entered as commands of which there are 18 (see Appendix A). Commands consist of a command name and, if necessary, parameter

values, the whole message being surrounded by double quotes. Logic includes the Boolean operators AND, OR, and AND NOT. A single search statement can be of almost any length, and can contain search terms from any or all searchable (indexed) categories of the unit record, combined together in any Boolean pattern, and in any sequence. Earlier search statements can be "nested" in later statements as single terms by use of the search statement number.

The interaction format is free-sequence; any command can be issued any time that the program will accept input. The eight routine program messages are presented in a long "composite" form, and can be shortened collectively or selectively to a short or a symbolic form. Both on-line and off-line explanations are available for all routine messages, commands, program features, and unit record contents. There are on-line tutorials, and an index display capability. Printing can be obtained on-line or off-line on the high speed printer, with air mail service. There is a command allowing the user to enter free-text comments that are stored for the system operators, a news command, and a capability to order hard copy backup from the terminal.[2]

THE PRESENT SERLINE ON-LINE SYSTEM

The following bibliographic information is contained in the data base for each serial title: title; journal title abbreviation; cross-reference; publisher name; city/state of publication; first-last issue; frequency; notes; locator codes; journal title code; sequence number; international standard serial number; coden; NLM catalog citation number; subject headings; language; country of publication; abstracting and indexing tags; year of publication; closed date of publication; closed entry indicator; NLM call number (for searchable and printable elements see listing below).

The locator information is carried in the form of a five character alpha-numeric code. The first two characters are numeric and identify the RML region to which a library belongs and the last three characters are an alphabetic code which specifically identifies a particular library within that region. Thus the locator code 01HMS indicates that the tile is held in the New England Region (Region I) and by the Francis A. Countway Library of Medicine (Harvard Medical School). Locator information for approximately 117 participating medical libraries is carried in the Serline Data Base. These Libraries represent the Regional Medical Libraries and other resource libraries which comprise the National Library of Medicine's Regional Medical Library Network.

Serline's prime function is to provide on-line bibliographic and locator information in support of the RML Network interlibrary loan activity. The system's secondary functions are to provide support for cooperative acquisitions and reference functions within the network.

Serline is now being tested by the National Library of Medicine for general use. It's general availability depends in part on the growth of Medline and the impact of charging for NLM on-line services. Hard

copy back-up of the serline Data Base will be provided. The form and method of distribution have not yet been determined.

SERLINE DATA ELEMENTS

CATEGORY QUALIFIER ABBREVIATION	CATEGORY NAMES	PRINTABLE	SEARCHABLE
TI	Title	X	X
JT	Journal Title Abbreviation	X	
PU	Publisher	X	X
PL	City/State of Publication	X	
FL	First-Last Issue	X	
FR	Frequency	X	
DN	NOTES	X	
R1	LOCATOR CODES - REGION 01	X	X
R2	LOCATOR CODES - REGION 02	X	X
R3	LOCATOR CODES - REGION 03	X	X
R4	LOCATOR CODES - REGION 04	X	X
R5	LOCATOR CODES - REGION 05	X	X
R6	LOCATOR CODES - REGION 06	X	X
R7	LOCATOR CODES - REGION 07	X	X
R8	LOCATOR CODES - REGION 08	X	X
R9	LOCATOR CODES - REGION 09	X	X
RT	LOCATOR CODES - REGION 10	X	X
RE	LOCATOR CODES - REGION 11	X	X
JC	Index Medicus Journal Title Code	X	X
UC	Sequence Number	X	
SN	International Standard Serial Number	X	X
CX	Coden	X	
NO	NLM Catalog Citation Number	X	
MH	Subject	X	X
LA	Language	X	X
CO	Country	X	X
AI	Abstract & Indexing Tag	X	X
CR	Cross Reference	X	X
YR	Year of Publication		X
CD	Closed Date of Publication		X
CY	Closed Entry		X
CN	Call Number	X	

RETRIEVAL FEATURES OF SERLINE

By "conversing" with the computer via an on-line terminal a user is able to retrieve almost instantaneously bibliographic information on ca 6500 biomedical serial titles and to locate these titles in any or all of the 117 participating libraries.

Titles and their cross-references are searchable in three ways: title search key; title words; and stringsearch.

The first of these methods is by the use of a search key developed by the Ohio Library College Center[3]. It is composed of the first three letters of the first significant word, followed by a slash (/), and then by the first letter of each of the next three words, all separated by slashes. Example: Title of *Bone and Joint Surgery* would be searched under BON/A/J/S.

The second method is by the use of keywords within the title or cross-reference field. All significant words within titles and cross-references have been added to the Index File, and are searchable; a list of "stop" words which have not been indexed is available. The significant words are designated by the category qualifier TITLE KEYWORD (TK) or CROSS REFERENCE KEYWORD (CK). In Serline's titles and cross-references, a word is defined as a set of characters which falls between blanks, numbers, or any punctuation other than the hyphen. You may search more than one word within a title by using the logical operators AND, OR, and AND NOT to connect the terms.

The third method is called stringsearch and gives the capability of searching character strings within titles or within other elements if the unit record. It has its greatest use in searching titles. Before performing a stringsearch, it is first necessary to execute a preliminary search using information appearing as index entries and then stringsearch the resultant citations. The initially retrieved citations are scanned in segments of thirty. After each group of thirty citations is scanned, the terminal user will be notified of the total citations scanned, the number of citations fulfilling his search, and then he will be asked whether he wishes to continue scanning or not. For a detailed explanation of title word searching and stringsearch see the National Library of Medicine's *Library Network/Medlars Technical Bulletin, March 1973.*[1]

Locator code is searchable both by region and by individual library. Example: 01# will retrieve all titles held by Region I. 01HMS will retrieve all titles held by The Francis A. Countway Library of Medicine. A locator code is not shown for NLM; titles held by NLM will be indicated by the presence of the NLM Call Number in the record.

A search statement can consist of any combination of entries from the searchable elements of the unit record, entered in any order and separated by the Boolean connectors AND, OR, and AND NOT.

The Serline Data Base serves as a bibliographic back up to the Medline Data Base.

SERLINE OPERATIONS

Communicating with the program: The user and the program interact alternately: first the program, then the user, etc.

The user: The user communicates with the program only after receiving the cue USER: (the word USER followed by a colon). The user can enter three types of messages:
(1) Search statements — searchable items entered alone or combined by AND, OR, AND NOT.
(2) Replies to questions — answers to the questions that the computer directs to the user. Choices of replies are furnished.
(3) Commands — instructions to the program requesting operations other than searching such as printing citations. Commands must always be entered in quotaion marks. Since the system assumes that an input is a search statement or a response to a question, it must be informed when this is not so. This information is conveyed by the use of the quotation marks.

The program: The program communicates with the user only after the cue PROG: (the abbreviation for program followed by a colon). The program gives four types of data:
(1) Postings — the number of citations matching a search statement request.
(2) Responses to commands — various responses to the user's commands, such as a printout of bibliographic or locator information.
(3) Questions — questions directed to the user which require a reply.
(4) Program messages — include error messages, SS 1/c? USER:, etc.

LOGIN AND PROGRAM GREETING

/LOGIN ....
THIS TERMINAL IS CONNECTED TO THE MEDLINE RETRIEVAL FILE SET HELLO FROM MEDLINE, THE MEDLINE AND SDILINE DATA BASES NOW CONTAIN MAY 1973 DATA. DO YOU WISH THE NEW-USER OR EXPERIENCED-USER FORMAT? TYPE N OR E AND STRIKE THE CARRIAGE RETURN KEY.

E

USER:

"FILE SERLINE"

PROG:

THIS TERMINAL IS CONNECTED TO THE SERLINE RETRIEVAL FILE SET

SS 1/C?

SAMPLE SEARCHES

The following interaction begins after the login and program greeting. In the following samples, the searches proceed making use of the various commands and search capabilities of Serline.

EXAMPLE: TITLE SEARCH KEY

SS   1/C?

USER:
NEW/E/J/O
PROG:

PSTG   (1)
SS   2/C?

USER:
"PRINT HOLDINGS"
PROG:

CN—W1 NE388
TI —NEW ENGLAND JOURNAL OF MEDICINE
R1—01HMS
R2—02COR 02CPS 02FDD 02MLC 02NJN 02NYA 02NYP
  02RUT 02SBR
R3—03CPP
R4—04HOW 04GTU 04GWU 04JHU 04MDB 04MCF 04TMC
  04VIR 04WVA
R5—05DET 05KEN 05LOU 05MIC 05MSU 05WSU
R6—06MIA 06ALA 06EMU 06FLO 06GEO 06MEH 06MIS
  06PUR 06SCA 06TEN 06VAN
R7—07ILL 07JCL 07MAY
R8—08COL 08CRU 08KAN 08MCO 08MEN 08NEB 08STL
  08UTA 08WSL 08WYO
R9—09CNM 09LNO 09LSU 09MEX 09OKL 09TEX 09TGA
  09TMA 09TSA 09TSW 09TUL
RT—10WAS
RE—11CIR 11CLA

EXAMPLE: TITLE WORD SEARCH

SS   3/C?

USER:
PREVENTIVE (TK)
PROG:

PSTG (2)
SS   4/C?

USER:
"PRINT FULL 1"
PROG:

CN —W1 BR634
TI —BRITISH JOURNAL OF PREVENTIVE AND SOCIAL
    MEDICINE
PL —LONDON
FL —7,1953—
DN—CONT OF BRITISH JOURNAL OF SOCIAL MEDICINE
R1 —01HMS
R2 —02COR 02CPS 02MLC 02NJN 02NYA 02RUT 02SBR
R3 —03CPP
R4 —04GWU 04JHU 04MDB 04TMC 04VIR 04WVA
R5 —05KEN 05LOU 05MIC 05MSU 05WSU
R6 —06MIA 06ALA 06EMU 06FLO 06MEH 06PUR 06SCA
    06TEN 06VAN
R7 —07ILL 07JCL 07MAY
R8 —08COL 08KAN 08MCO 08NEB 08UTA 08WSL
R9 —09LNO 09MEX 09OKL 09TEX 09TGA 09TMA 09TSA
    09TSW 09TUL
RT —10WAS
RE —11CIR 11CLA
JC —BIC
UC —123676000
SN —00071242
CX —BJPVA
MH—PUBLIC HEALTH
MH—SOCIAL MEDICINE
LA —ENGLISH
CO —UNITED KINGDOM
AI —IM
AI —MED

EXAMPLE: STRINGSEARCH

SS   1/C?

USER:
JOU/O/T/A
PROG:

PSTG (33)
SS   2/C?

USER:
TS (TI) : PREVENTIVE DENTISTRY :
PROG:

(30) RECORDS SEARCHED AND (1) QUALIFIED. CONTINUE SEARCHING?
(YES/NO)

USER:
YES
PROG:

PSTG (1)
SS   3/C?

USER:
"PRINT HOLDINGS"
PROG:

TI —JOURNAL OF THE AMERICAN SOCIETY FOR PREVENTIVE DENTISRY
R1—01TUF
R3—03PED
R7—07ILL
R8—08WSL
RT—10WAS

EXAMPLE: ABRIDGED INDEX MEDICUS TITLES* HELD BY
WAYNE STATE UNIVERSITY IN REGION V.

PROG:

SS   1/C?

USER:
AIM (AI) AND 05WSU
PROG:

PSTG (95)   *The SERLINE Test Data Base contains 97 of the 100 AIM Titles.

EXAMPLE: ABRIDGED INDEX MEDICUS TITLES NOT HELD
BY WAYNE STATE UNIVERSITY.

USER:
AIM (AI) AND NOT 05WSU
PROG:

PSTG (2)
SS   3/C?

USER:
"PRINT HOLDINGS"
PROG:

CN—W1 CL797
TI —CLINICAL TOXICOLOGY
R1—01HMS
R2—02CPS 02NJN 02NYA
R3—03CPP
R4—04GWU 04JHU 04MDB 04TMC 04VIR 04WVA
R5—05KEN 05MIC 05MSU
R6—06MIA 06ALA 06FLO 06SCA
R7—07ILL 07IND
R8—08COL 08MCO 08NEB
R9—09CNM 09LSU 09MEX 09TEX 09TGA 09TSW
RT—10WAS
RE—11CLA

CN—W1 RH39
TI —RHEUMATOLOGY AND PHYSICAL MEDICINE
R1—01HMS
R2—02COR 02CPS 02NJN 02NYA 02RUT 02SBR
R3—03CPP

```
R4—04MDB 04TMC
R5—05KEN
R6—06MIA 06ALA 06EMU 06FLO 06GEO 06MIS 06SCA
R7—07ILL 07JCL 07MAY
R9—09LNO  09LSU  09MEX  09OKL  09TEX  09TSA  09TSW
    09TUL
RT—10WAS
RE—11CIR 11CLA
```

EXAMPLE: MEDLINE TITLES NOT HELD IN THE DISTRICT OF COLUMBIA (04) i.e. NOT HELD BY HOWARD UNIVERSITY MEDICAL AND DENTAL LIBRARY (HOW), GEORGETOWN UNIVERSITY MEDICAL CENTER (GTU), AND GEORGE WASHINGTON UNIVERSITY MEDICAL LIBRARY (GWU).

SS   1/C?

USER:
04HOW OR 04GTU OR 04GWU
PROG:

PSTG (1395)
SS   2/C?

USER:
MED (AI) AND NOT 1
PROG:

PSTG (399)
SS   3/C?

USER:
"PRINT"
PROG:

CN—W1 AC749
TI —ACTA ANAESTHESIOLOGICA BELGICA
FL—1,1950
DN—1-2 PUB IN ACTA CHIRURGICA BELGICA. 3 PUB AS SUPP

.
.
.
.
.

CN—W1 ZH425

TI —ZHURNAL VYSSHEI NERVNOI DEIATELNOSTI IMENI I.P. PAVLOVA
FL—1,1951

APPENDIX A — LIST OF ELHILL COMMANDS

COMMAND NAME	ABBR.	FUNCTION
EXPLAIN	EX	Allows user to obtain on-line explanation of any command or program message.
VERSION	VERS	Allows user to set routing messages to one of three levels: symbolic, short, or full.
FIND	FD	Allows user to enter a search statement without receiving the readiness cue.
NEIGHBOR	NBR	Retrieves index terms that are alphabetic neighbors of the search term and indicates the number of postings for each.
DIAGRAM	DIAG	Allows user to trace the structure of search statements, especially when search statements have been formed by combination of other search statements.
ERASEBAK	ERSBK	Allows user to erase some specified number of search statements.
ERASEALL	ERSLL	Erases all previous search statements.
RESTART	RST	Allows user to erase all stored records of interactions with the program and start over again.
PRINT	PRT	Causes program to print out information desired. User has many options such as on- and off-line, format, elements to printed, relevance, etc. The print format options in Serline are print full, print, and print holdings.

RENAME	RNM	Allows user to designate any arbitrary name for any command.
STOP	STOP	Allows user to stop the program at any point during the operation.
*TREE	TREE	Causes thesaurus display of terms hierarchically related to specified term.
*MESHNO	MNO	Provides MeSH classification number of specified term.
COMMENT	COMMENT	Allows user to type in comments which are stored for system personnel.
ORDER	ORDER	Allows user to order hard copy back-up from terminal.
NEWS	NEWS	Provides user with announcements, etc.
RESTACK	RSTK	Causes the latest search statement to be renumbered to SSN 1, and all other statements to be erased.

*Not applicable in Serline.

BIBLIOGRAPHY

1. Greehey, B. L., and Bahlman, L. J. "New capabilities in Medline," *Library Network/Medlars Technical Bulletin*, (47) pp. 11-20, March 1973.

2. Katter, R. V., and McCarn, D. B., "AIM-TWX — An Experimental On-Line Bibliographic Retrieval System," in *Interactive Bibliographic Search: The User/Computer Interface*, ed. D. E. Walker, pp. 121-141. Montvale, New Jersey: AFIPS Press. 1971.

3. Long, P. L., and Kilgour, F. G. "A truncated search key title index," *Journal of Library Automation*, 5(1) pp. 17-20, March 1972.

4. Sawyers, E. J. "Union list development: control of the serial literature," *Bulletin of the Medical Library Association*, 60(3) pp. 427-431, July 1972.

THE PROBLEMS OF ENTERING A COMPUTERIZED SERIALS NETWORK
OR
THE VALIDITY OF MURPHY'S LAW

Priscilla Mayden

Bringing about change in the organization is a continuing and difficult responsibility of the administrator. Change, to accomplish the maximum benefit, must be done with minimal disruption. The administrator's job is to gain compliance for change from those above him in the hierarchy and more importantly from his staff who will be carrying out the change. Then, as a final test, he must achieve acceptance for the change from the public.

Change is essential to the effectiveness of any organization. Progress is growth, if not in size in wisdom, and growth is change. Yet, there is common human preference for maintaining the status quo. Outside of the innovating group, resistance is a natural response for the human beings that comprise the organization.

Change, even change for the better, creates stress and demands an uncomfortable coping behavior from the individual. T. H. Holmes[1], in a recent popular study on social readjustment, has compiled a list of 43 common life events involving change and has placed them on a rating scale. These life stress situations, from the extraordinary like sudden death of a spouse, to the commonplace, like Christmas, have each been assigned a value. He found that regardless of age, sex or economic status, these changes, even pleasurable ones, produce measurable stress. Clustered in the middle of this scale somewhere between "trouble with in-laws" and "taking out a mortgage" are "business adjustments" "changes in responsibilities at work" a "revision of habits" and "trouble with the boss."

Automating the library's serials system can involve all these changes for the individual library staff member. People naturally fear the confusion that may follow change. Automation, particularly, is still an unknown and therefore a threat. Will it make my job harder? Can I ever learn to understand how it works? Will it make me feel stupid in front of others? Will it downgrade my job or eliminate it altogether? Even if a radical change like computerization is done expertly and well, it is bound to produce some of this stress for staff and public. If it is done poorly and without regard for the human element, the coping behavior that follows can tear the organization apart.

From my own experience in entering our library into the PHILSOM serials system, I believe the impact of a system on a functioning library staff may be the most important planning element for the administrator to consider.

The administrator, with his own enthusiasm and high personal motivation for improvement and progress can easily overlook what may happen with the people down the line. In the excitement of pressing on it is easy to misread all the danger signals.

Our decision to enter PHILSOM was not made by any known sound principle of management. There was no study group formed at the operating level to consider it and its alternatives, and there should have been. There was no cost analysis and comparison, except for some hasty arithmetic on the back of an envelope, and there should have been. The library staff, as such, was not involved until it was a *fait accompli.* They should have been, they weren't, and that was nearly fatal. The management decision instead was made intuitively, perhaps impulsively. We did have complete and well founded faith in the Washington University staff and in PHILSOM itself. In fact, we believed in it so thoroughly ourselves that we were completely convinced that the library staff, once informed, would see at a glance its many benefits and embrace it eagerly, too. Alas, how naive (which is to say, how stupid!)

Those of you who direct or work in absolutely systems-perfect libraries managed by yourselves or by a director who walks on water or at least leaps over tall buildings with a single bound may have trouble in understanding our problems. Those who do not, may take some small comfort in knowing that others, too, make foolish blunders. We did indeed enter our library into that excellent computerized system, the PHILSOM serials network, but we did it making every possible mistake and every wrong decision except *one.* That was the decision to do it! We've never been sorry, never looked back, until now, and are happier every day with the outcome. But there have been a lot of tears and travail in between, beginning with the day my assistant and I came back from St. Louis, gathered our startled staff together and said, "Hey, fellas, guess what we've done!"

When Washington University sent a representative to orient and train the staff, enthusiasm was high — at least we thought it was. The clerks who would be working with the system appeared interested and eager to learn. Others not directly involved were quiet and skeptical.

The public services staff sat through the day's training tight-lipped and polite and returned to their desks unconvinced. They were the oldest members of the staff both chronologically and in length of service. They were the ones who would be facing the public for the next two years, explaining and placating. They were the least involved at the beginning, but had the most to lose if we failed and they knew it.

Perhaps a word here about this particular library and staff would be appropriate. When we entered PHILSOM in April 1970, our library contained about 70,000 volumes and had 1,350 active journal subscriptions, small by most medical school standards. We were severly hampered by lack of space and a dismal sub-basement location where we were to be housed temporarily until our new building was completed.

We had just emerged after a long governance battle, independent at last from the administration of our parent university library. That was a plus.

There were three professional librarians besides the Director; a Reference Librarian, a Cataloger, and a Technical Services Librarian. Since technical services had been handled for us by the main library, the non-professional staff had traditionally been largely untrained student assistants on time-card wages. Our new freedom had not yet produced a realistic budget and our staff was still small of necessity. We did have three full-time, capable, mature assistants in public services. The entire staff was enthusiastic about our new autonomy and anxious that we do well on our own.

Separating our collections and moving came first in 1967. Two years later when the administrative separation occurred, we took over our own ordering, processing and record keeping from the main library. Proper serials control was becoming a serious problem and was reaching crisis proportions in late 1969. The integrity of fiscal and binding records had suffered in the move, and even our own Kardex records had deteriorated. In the separation, important subscriptions were somehow dropped, standing orders vanished and our attempts to back and fill seemed to produce only more duplicates, bad feeling and chaos.

We knew that our system would have to be improved, modified or totally changed. The least disruptive approach was to try to improve, and try we did, to shape up the old system, clean up our records and fly right. The details of this reform movement are not too enlightening nor the outcome very inspiring. We made some progress but it was like climbing a mountain of mashed potatoes.

When the opportunity to join PHILSOM was offered, we were more than ready for a real change. We knew we would have to establish control of our system by computer eventually. To have the chance to do it by the simple act of joining a network with an on-going, proven system was irresistible. PHILSOM, with more than ten years of carefully documented research and development behind it, seemed to promise instant order out of chaos with all the scary risks removed — the answer to our prayers! These were our objectives for the system:

1) Improved service to our patrons (which is also the first objective of the library itself)
2) Increased control over all aspects of the serials operation, particularly fiscal control.
3) Cost reduction through savings in man hours.

We drew up a plan for entering titles by category — our most used core journals to go first, and the dead titles last, with target dates for each goal in between.

With the preliminary training completed, we were ready to begin.

One of the most attractive characteristics of PHILSOM is that the system is designed to be used by people with no special knowledge or expertise in computer technology. This definition described my own

capabilities very well. As Director, I had taken the usual quickie courses, attended workshops and done some reading, but until then I had had no experience, no real life contact whatever with the computer field. For this I depended entirely on an assistant, much more experienced and knowledgeable than I, to undertake direction of the project. She brought tremendous drive and enthusiasm to the PHILSOM project at the outset. If she had remained with us even through our first year, our technical and staff training problems might by then have been resolved. But she did not, and in July 1970, four months after our first titles had been entered, we had received our second print out, she had left us to accept another position. To add to the crisis, the two clerical assistants who were trained to do daily PHILSOM operations, and who, as we were soon to discover, really understood very little of what they were doing, went into panic and resigned without notice a month later.

In the meantime, I was deeply involved elsewhere with the planning, programming and building of a new library building. I had made no attempt to learn more about PHILSOM in those four months and knew even less about it in July than I had known in March. I was helpless as a kitten in trying to avert disaster or later to put it all back together. Incoming journals began to pile up. I was apprehensive, but not too alarmed, as I felt that we could rely temporarily at least on the old manual system to carry us through until we could get a new project director and train new clerks.

It was at this point that a new nightmare began. Despite all caveats in the literature and our expressed intent to maintain the manual system until we were secure, we found the old system had been dropped when the changeover was made. As each record was entered in PHILSOM, the Kardex record had been destroyed. Lack of space and man-power had supposedly made maintenance of dual systems an impossibility. But the additional motivation for eliminating the Kardex had been to quickly overcome resistance to the new system by abruptly severing dependence on the old one. Well, we had broken the first commandment of automation and discovered the hard way that the penalty would be steep.

We made a frantic call for help to St. Louis asking them to grant us another consulting and training visit. A library assistant with quite unrelated responsibilities but some knowledge of the system and an interest in seeing it work volunteered to take charge temporarily. We hired a new clerk and shakily started over. In the summer of 1970 there was little possibility of locating and attracting a librarian with computer experience to come to Utah to take over.

Although we lived through two complete serials staff turnovers in three months, by December, we were beginning to recover.

After a long search we found locally a qualified clerical assistant who liked the PHILSOM system and wanted to work with it. He was a graduate student, in another field, but with extensive data processing

experience in the army. He needed a part-time job and liked the sound of ours. He studied the system carefully on his own, using the manual and benefiting greatly from the second visit from network headquarters. Slowly, he began to solve some of our problems. He suggested keypunching our own data correction, producing our own daily lists and duplicating our receipt card decks. He began to clean up the bad data that we had entered previously and to restore integrity to the record. A few months later, we were beginning to reply with confidence to letters of inquiry from other libraries who were considering coming into the system. Our new expert understood the programming well and the technical side of the system. We had come a long way, but the light at the end of the tunnel still eluded us.

Meanwhile, back at the reference and circulation desks the mood had gone from one of total disbelief when we entered PHILSOM, to open anger at the end of year one, to a kind of sullen resignation by the middle of year two. Although improved service to the public had supposedly been our first objective, we had paid only the briefest lip service to that commendable goal. Our public services staff had been thoroughly indoctrinated with the library's service-first policy. They knew better than any of us that no aspect of service was more vital to the public than serials. Yet the new system had been adopted without their advice or consent. They had not been asked for their opinion of a computerized system beforehand, only told of its supposed virtues and the great benefit they could expect once it was working. In their eyes of course, these benefits had never arrived.

At the beginning when they were openly angry, we were too busy to listen. Their complaints were an annoyance and a rebuke. When the protests stopped, we thought at last they had accepted the system and seen the light. Nothing could have been farther from the truth.

Roger Vergin[2], speaking of the impact of computers on the industrial organizations, found the highest acceptance of computerization was found among those employees involved in designing the system and planning the changeover. Resistance was highest, naturally, among those left out, whose responsibilities were downgraded or curtailed by computerization. This could truly be said of the public services staff and the public itself.

When we finally did listen we learned that the public services staff lost all confidence in the new system at the time when they were deprived of the manually-kept record. The substituion of the early PHILSOM printouts provided highly unreliable data. The public hated them. The staff hated them more. Even though they knew the quality would improve they could not be reconciled to the loss of what they saw as their accountability to the public. No longer was it possible to tell a patron after a glance at the Kardex whether the latest issue of a journal was in; when it could be expected; what action had been taken to replace a missing issue; whether a volume had been bound; whether it was at the bindery and when it was due back; the year of a single

volume in a run; how many issues per volume, or how many volumes per year. It left them feeling helpless and stupid not to be able to respond to simple inquiries without going to the shelves. The public had come to expect answers and was not impressed with computer sheets that did not seem to supply them. Had these valuable and knowledgeable members of the staff been taken into the planning at the beginning, these difficulties could have been anticipated and met at the outset. All of these problems have been overcome now, and the system is supplying more information than the old manual system — like subject and language lists, location information, and accurate title change and historical information never easily available before. But that all came later. In the meantime, the system had to be by-passed in order to serve the public properly. The public services staff had been carefully instructed on one point — never to attribute mistakes in the record to our inability to locate material to "the computer" as is frequently done by clerks in department stores and hospitals when explaining billing errors. To their credit, they never did, although the temptation to pass the buck to this mechanical scapegoat must have been strong at times. But the public, conditioned by experience elsewhere, knew better and did its own attributing. Many preferred asking for help rather than using a serials list anyway, and merely continued to do so.

It was not until a new assistant became our PHILSOM manager at the beginning of the third year that we began to wipe out these last pockets of staff resistance. The system was running well and he had been thoroughly trained on the job as back-up for his predecessor. He realized soon after taking over, however, that although the system was still far from perfect, no one was complaining and he was getting no suggestions for changing or improving it. Discreet inquiry revealed that those who did not have to come in contact with PHILSOM were avoiding it entirely. The public services staff was simply by-passing it as completely as possible. The public did not understand it and rarely used it. Only the technical services staff was really benefiting from it. He began at once on his own initiative a highly personal campaign to educate every member of the staff to the system and its capabilities, requiring each one to do hands-on coding and data input. This was followed by frequent staff meeting sessions for questions and feedback. With his own enthusiasm for PHILSOM and his considerable teaching skills, he was able to turn the tide. Everyone understands, uses and relies on PHILSOM now. But, sometimes even success has its drawbacks. Next week our efficient PHILSOM supervisor leaves us to come to St. Louis to become manager for the entire system. When our most conservative circulation assistant inspected the first PHILSOM fiscal data report to appear last week and exclaimed "this is really wonderful," we knew we had made it at last.

C. K. Bauer[3], in a recent issue of *Special Libraries*, recounts the ten years of automation experience in the Technical Information Department of Lockheed Georgia Company. He says, "In retrospect, one may

seriously question whether the progress made in so many steps, compounded by confusion, delays and high cost factors really served the cause well. It is clear that, were the job to be done all over again, surely a better course could have been charted because of the lessons that have been learned." He enumerates nine lessons that Lockheed learned in ten years. Here are five that we have learned in three, many of them similar to his on a smaller scale.

Lesson No. 1:
To enter a system successfully the library administrator himself must have at least a working knowledge of the computerized system. This is essential for wise planning, commitment of resources, continuity, and the ability to make informed decisions and take quick action when necessary.

Lesson No. 2:
Staffing should provide for every person professional or clerical, working with the system to have the back-up of one other person who understands the system and has a working knowledge of the job. This may be difficult on a small and over-committed staff, but is essential.

Lesson No. 3:
When converting to the new system the manual or previously used system should be maintained during the transition.

Lesson No. 4:
No commitment should be made until a set of objectives and a detailed plan for achieving them, including an adequate budget for unforseen emergencies, has been prepared.

Lesson No. 5:
Participation of all the staff in the decision making, the planning, training and at every step of the implementation is essential.

Once the system is operational, provision for continuous feedback from staff and public users will keep it responsive to needs and constantly improving.

BIBLIOGRAPHY

1. HOLMES, T. H. and Rake, R. H.: The social readjustment rating scale. *Journal of Psychosomatic Research*, Vol. 11:213-218, 1967.

2. VERGIN, Roger: Computer induced organization changes, In Wortman, M. S. *Emerging Concepts in Management.* Macmillan, 1969, (p. 318-330)

3. BAUER, Charles K.: Automation and its lessons. *Special Libraries*, Vol. 63:47-52, 1972

THE PHILSOM NETWORK: THE COORDINATOR'S VIEWPOINT

Virginia Feagler

As Mr. Johnson said, each of us on the panel will be talking about the Philsom system from a particular viewpoint. I am currently the Director and Coordinator of the PHILSOM network. This morning I would like to briefly describe the PHILSOM system, explain my responsibilities as the coordinator and discuss the problems encountered and some of the advantages of networks.

PHILSOM, an acronym for "Periodical Holdings in Library School of Medicine," is an automated record control system that is run on the batch mode. It is currently used by seven libraries: the Washington University School of Medicine Library, and the Medical School Libraries of the Universities of Utah, Missouri, St. Louis, Texas (at San Antonio), Illinois, and the National Institutes of Health Library. At this time the data base contains approximately 8300 titles, both current and non-current.

Journals are, in general, entered by the title and are alphabetized in word order. Each title on the PHILSOM file has two distinct parts: basic data and location data. Basic information for each entry includes the full title of the journal, the bibliographic history if needed, and cross references. In addition, if it is a current journal, the publication information is entered — i.e. how frequently the journal is published, the current volume and issue being published and the number of issues per volume — as well as subject, language and Index Medicus codes. All of this is the same for every library holding the journal title. On the other hand, location data consists of information which is unique to each library, e.g. the particular volumes and issues owned, how it is bound and where it is shelved. This must be supplied by each library, since obviously we would not know how each individual library handles the title.

The PHILSOM master file is updated once a month with new titles and changes to titles already established in the file, including the computer produced check-in cards which update each library's holdings statement. The network libraries receive automatically each month an updated list of their journal titles with specific holdings for each title, i.e. the particular volumes and issues owned by the library. This list contains both the basic data, i.e. bibliographic information for the titles and the location data, i.e. information unique to each library. The system can also produce a variety of other information: a list of missed issues by vendor or publisher, an overdue warning if a journal issue has not been received for a specific amount of time, check-in cards or receipt cards for the journal issues which should be published that month, notices for journal titles which are ready for binding and fiscal reports which totals the amount of money expended during the past

month, as well as a list of titles which need to be renewed within the fiscal year.

The libraries in the network can receive on request lists of titles by subject, by language, or by shelving location within their own library. Libraries in the network can also request extra copies of their list of journal titles. There is an additional cost for any of these demand lists, for extra copies of any regular monthly output or for any other special work.

My responsibilities as coordinator of the PHILSOM network are varied and run the gamut from day-to-day routines, e.g. making sure that the data submitted by member libraries is edited promptly, to teaching the personnel of a new network library how to code its manual records so they can be entered in the PHILSOM file. As I said earlier, a title on the file has two parts — the general information or basic data and the information unique to each library or location data. All data, except that on the computer produced check-in cards, is edited before it is keypunched. The basic data, however, is checked more carefully than is the location data, because, as I said before, we have no way of knowing where the other library shelves the title or how it binds it.

When a title new to the Philsom file is received from a participating library, it is checked against the master file of the data base of the *Union Catalog of Medical Periodicals* (U.C.M.P.) published by the Medical Library Center of New York. Our reasons for choosing it as an authority will be discussed later. If we cannot identify the title in U.C.M.P., we send it to New York for determination of title entry. Once the entry is established, the publication information, i.e. how often the journal is published, the current volume and issue being published, how many issues per volume, is examined to determine that the data is coded correctly. Subject codes are verified to insure that they are valid and reasonable subject headings. For example, we do not want to submit a subject code of "Orthopedics" if the journal obviously is about "Obstetrics and Gynecology." The abbreviated title, which will appear on the receipt card, is checked against the abbreviations used by *Index Medicus* or the *National Clearinghouse for Periodical Title Word Abbreviations.*

Bibliographic information is also verified. Our authority for bibliographic history is again the *Union Catalog of Medical Periodicals.* If the bibliographic information cannot be verified there, we use other references tools, such as *New Serial Titles, Union List of Serials,* and *Vital Notes.* Since we have insisted that all PHILSOM entries conform to an outside authority, we enter cross references requested by cooperating libraries readily. We do, however, ask for some kind of verification for a cross reference request.

Basic data changes to titles already on the file are examined carefully and must be accompanied by some kind of verification, e.g. a notice from the publisher indicating that the title changed.

The information which is unique to each library — that is, the

location data — cannot be checked for accuracy, as is the basic information, so we accept what is sent to us. When location data is submitted, however, it must include the numeric title code, the library location code, and the set title code. The holdings statement must be formatted as specified in the *PHILSOM Documentation, 2nd edition*. An action code, which determines if a title is current or non-current for a particular library, is mandatory. These particular items we can and do check.

Communicating with the participating libraries is also an important function. It is not enough for us to know what we are doing, that the data is being processed, or that a program problem is being corrected. The other libraries must know too, and they need this information more often than once a month when they receive their outputs. For that reason, once a week we produce on our document writer a list of basic data changes and new titles which have been checked and keypunched that week. Included with the basic data listing is the PHILSOM *Newsletter* containing answers to general questions posed by the users, status reports of network projects, and questionnaires on matters of general interest and particular problems. We send most of the monthly output to the libraries by airfreight, and we, TWX all the libraries in the network to tell them when the monthly output was dispatched. As soon as we have the flight information, usually the following day, we TWX the flight number, day and time of arrival, and the package number so that it can be picked up by the library, if it wishes or traced if necessary. Unique questions or problems are dealt with on an individual basis. We try to keep everyone well informed so that the left hand knows what the right hand is doing.

Although checking the data and communicating with the participating libraries are the Coordinator's two most time consuming jobs, teaching the personnel in other libraries about the Philsom system is no less important. If the librarians and the assistants understand how to code and how to use the monthly outputs, then the information will be coded correctly and will, therefore take less time to check.

The PHILSOM update is scheduled to run at the Computer Center the third Friday of each month. When the monthly update is complete, the Computer Center sorts the printout by library. At that time we are notified that the update is complete. We then pick up approximately 16 boxes of printout; this has to be packed and sent to the other network libraries. Arranging and coordinating this aspect of the PHILSOM network is also part of my job.

When the member libraries request program changes, I am the liasion between the network and the Director of Machine Projects. He keeps me informed of the status of various projects and I, in turn, tell the network libraries. So as you can see the job of coordinator is varied.

During the past few minutes, I have briefly described the PHILSOM system and my responsibilities as coordinator. Nothing, however, is free of problems and the same thing is true with networks. I like to separate

the problems into two broad categories — the first one is oriented around attitudes, and sometimes misconceptions, held by individual librarians about computers, while the second general area deals with problems which affect the entire network. The success or failure of an automated system is largely determined by the library personnel who use it as part of their daily operation. Trying to sell the PHILSOM system to the serials personnel of an incoming library can be one of my most difficult tasks. Before a library decides to enter the network, we encourage it to examine the system carefully and to evaluate if PHILSOM can meet the needs of that particular library. When the final decision has been made, the serials personnel in the "new" library should feel fairly secure that the program operates well and does what it is designed to do. Once PHILSOM has been accepted by a library, it is necessary to teach the serials personnel how to code their manual records and how to use the various monthly outputs. At this point the library staff's attitudes toward automation become obvious. Some people are afraid of computers. To them a computer is an enormous machine over which they have no control. Since they were not involved in the planning and implementation stages of the system, they do not always realize that the computer only carries out the tasks which other librarians have decided it could do better and faster than a human. On the other hand, some library personnel view an automated system as a panacea — it will solve all the nitty-gritty problems which characterize serial publications without any work on their part. During the training periods for new libraries, I try to use a realistic approach to the PHILSOM system to show what it can do, what it could do if the program were changed, and what it cannot do. I emphasize that PHILSOM will give them rapid access to the problems, but it cannot solve all the problems. Manual checking will still be a necessity as, for example, determining if a claim for an overdue or late journal issue is warranted.

The training of personnel does not end with the intensive 2 day introductory session. When personnel changes occur within a library, it is sometimes necessary to have the new staff member come here for an individual training period.

I have discussed in depth the first general problem area, attitudes and misconceptions, and now I will move on to the second — problems which affect all the member libraries. Probably the major one is the necessity of standardization, particularly the way journals will be entered on the PHILSOM file. Being a serials librarian myself, I readily understand that probably no two serial librarians would enter a journal the same way. Each of us seems to have a unique way of evaluating how a title should be entered. In a network situation, this could cause chaos, as well as unreasonable growth of the file. In order to relieve ourselves of some of the responsibility for correct title entry and to keep from offending any of the member libraries, it was decided that an outside authority for correct entry in the Philsom file was needed. Since the

Union Catalog of Medical Periodicals (U.C.M.P.) produced by the Medical Library Center of New York has the largest data base of medical periodicals, we chose it as our authority. Once the decision had been made to use the same entries as U.C.M.P. did, the ramifications were enormous. All new titles, of course, had to conform to the U.C.M.P. entry. Any existing discrepancies for titles already on the file had to be identified and changed. This was no small task. Each entry in PHILSOM was checked against the *Union Catalog of Medical Periodicals* and all differences were noted, including titles which were not listed in the printed copies. The participating libraries in the network helped us with the identification part of the project. The next phase consisted of changing all entries which differed and this took approximately 6 months to complete. We also found there were approximately 1200 titles which were not listed in the printed copies of U.C.M.P., so we had to check these against the printout of the U.C.M.P. master file. Although the main portion of the project is now complete, we are still finding entries in Philsom which do not conform to U.C.M.P.

Of course, problems with the computer and the program cannot be overlooked. The program, in general, functions well, but there are always a few disasters which are flukes. Unfortunately, the computer can be a tempermental animal, and when it does go down, we are at its mercy. This was evidenced during the April update and consequently, the output was two days later than usual. These problems, although infrequent, are extremely difficult to explain to the member libraries.

The distance of the participating libraries, except for St. Louis University Medical Library, is another problem. It takes several days for data or check in cards to reach us. The library sending the information does not know when, or for that fact, if we ever receive it. Similarly, when the monthly output is boxed and dispatched, it takes 1-2 days for the other libraries to receive it although here they know from our TWX's when we sent it.

Most of these difficulties and annoyances are lessened, however, if good communication exists between the network center and the participating libraries. Keeping everyone informed about what is happening, as well as asking them for their ideas, is essential. When the PHILSOM network started in 1969, it consisted of three libraries — ours, the University of Utah Medical Library and the University of Missouri Medical Library. We did not realize how important it was for the other two libraries to know what was happening to their data or what we were doing about various problems. Both of these libraries were patient and fortunately did not become greatly upset with our mistakes. In December, 1970 it became apparent that Utah and Missouri needed more from us than their monthly outputs, so we instituted the *PHILSOM Newsletter* and started listing the basic information which had been submitted and keypunched during the past week. As more libraries entered the network, it was even more apparent

that we had to keep them informed. We also decided that a library should know if its data was changed by us for some reason. When we have made changes, we return to the cognizant library a zeroxed copy of the data sheet with the change noted and our reason for making it.

In spite of our best efforts, mistakes will happen. When a mistake is made, it helps us if one of the libraries notifies us. As in departments in a library, communication is not totally the responsibility of the central office. We must keep the serial librarians in the participating libraries informed. It is their job, however, to keep us informed and especially to pass the information to the other staff members in the library. Without this, our efforts have little effect.

Now that I have talked about the problems of a network operation, I ought to mention the other side, namely the advantages of a network. First of all, a participating library in a network does not have to worry about scheduling computer time. It seems that libraries, in general, are not a high priority job when it comes to a Computer Center, so scheduling a monthly update can be an obstacle to automating. Nor does a library need to employ its own programmer or systems analyst or worry about maintenance of the program; when it is part of a network, these problems are handled by the network coordinating library.

Another advantage of the PHILSOM system is the union copy produced in triplicate each month. The union copy includes the bibliographic information, i.e. the basic data, for every current and non-current title on the file, as well as the unique information, or location data of each network library. Each participating library receives a union copy every three months. This list is especially useful to the serials section as a means for identifying a new publication as one already established on the file, as well as being a guide for claiming overdue materials. For example, if one library in the network has received an issue of a particular title and another has not, then a claim is probably necessary. This enables the library to keep its serial holdings current. Our interlibrary loan section uses the Philsom union copy to locate other libraries from whom to borrow materials.

With the federal budget in a state of flux and costs increasing, all of us in libraries are concerned about funding. How to cut costs is plaguing all of us. Probably one of the largest budget items in a library, after personnel costs, is the book budget. If the amount of money funded for buying books and renewing subscriptions is drastically reduced, what will we do? Cooperative acquisitions among libraries may become a necessity. We will need to know the titles to which other libraries are currently subscribing and the titles which are duplicated in several libraries. For example, of the seven libraries currently participating in the Philsom system, four of them are participating libraries in the Mid-Continental Regional Medical Library network. If current subscriptions do need to be dropped, we now have the necessary information with which we could implement a cooperative serial

acquisition policy among these four libraries.

Throughout my discussion about the PHILSOM system, a recurrent theme has been communication — for example, the role it plays in my job and problems that can arise when the participating libraries are not well informed. Now I would like to emphasize another aspect of communication — the exchanging of ideas among librarians from various parts of the country. In October, 1972 the first PHILSOM workshop was held at Washington University School of Medicine Library. It was the first time we had assembled as a group. At least one representative from each participating network library was present, as well as members from the Washington University Computer Center. The afternoon session was devoted to problems encountered by the users of the PHILSOM system and their ideas for improving the network. I think everyone benefited — we found out more about the user side of the network, and the participating libraries began to understand the problems that we encouter and why our demand for verification is necessary. We discussed problems common to all serials and learned from one another. We have now determined to make this an annual affair, and we have a steering committee for each year. The chance to interact with other librarians, bound by a common tie, in this case the PHILSOM network, stimulates and challenges the people involved and thus, enables us to view our job more objectively and creatively!

THE PHILSOM NETWORK: A PROGRAMMER/ANALYST'S VIEW

Neil Falvey

From a programmer's viewpoint this system does two things:
(1) *Converts inputs to outputs.* More specifically, converts machine readable inputs to presentation output. By presentation output, I mean printed output suitable for human viewing.
(2) *Stores data over time.* The inputs from one month's run must be available on subsequent months. In the Philsom system, the input in its original form and its side effects must remain available as input to the next monthly run.

These two major functions should be orthogonal to each other. That is, when addressing ones attention to file maintenance (the storage function) one should not have to concern oneself with system output. Conversely, when addressing oneself to the appearance and content of any specific presentation output one does not want to be distracted with concern over data input and file maintenance. This concept represents a somewhat more advanced way of thinking than prevailed when this system was conceived. Many of the problems and frustration experienced during the original development and the early years of operation can be traced directly to the fusing of these two functions.

Before continuing, I would like to take a moment to review the properties of a computer, in particular those properties that are important in the development of a large information processing system.

A computer is *very fast*. The model we use at Washington University is capable of performing a quarter of a million operations in a second. (by operations we mean the addition or subtraction of two numbers, or the choice between a larger or smaller value, or the transfer of a fragment of information from one point in the system to another). If we count to four slowly, one million small steps toward a problem solution will have occurred.

A computer is also *extremely accurate*. An internal error occurs roughly once a month. These errors are usually detected by the computer itself. At Washington University, there has not been a single authenticated case of an undetected error in the eight years we have used the IBM 360.

By now you are probably asking yourselves, with speed and accuracy such as this, how is it possible for computer-based systems to produce tardy results and the great number errors which we see with such alarming regularity?

To gain some insight into the problem let us look at how a computer solves problems. A computer moves from the input state to the target state in a series of very small steps. Each step is in complete isolation from the remainder of the problem. A rough analogy might go something like this. We commission an artist to paint the Grand

Canyon. However, we handicap him by enclosing him in a paper container. This container has a tiny hole in it so he can see out. The hole is just large enough for him to view one square inch of surface at a time. Needless to say, a painting made under these conditions will suffer greatly from lack of context and perspective. This same order of perspective reduction is a basic property of all computer systems.

To compound the problem still further, the computer is a one-dimensional device. Each step must follow the other in an unvarying sequence. To be sure, all of the program is not used by each transaction. Program control hops from one point to another depending on the requirements for a given transaction. For example, the receipt cards in the Philsom system skip over the part of the program required by the header cards and vice-versa. Nevertheless the essential sequence is the same, each action simply skips over the parts of the program which do not apply. Contrast this with the way in which a human approaches a problem or performs a task. People start with a trial sequence of thought, then another, and another, skipping around partial solutions rejecting some, continuing with others until we find the proper thread and are able to unravel the problem. Or, if performing a routine task, the human worker is endowed with some measure of judgement and will apply it to the job. Million dollar payroll checks will not be issued, or purchase orders will not be typed for a single pencil in a non-automated system. The human workman always has his perspective with him, the computer does only what is programmed and then only in the most simple way.

To summarize; the task of the programmer/analyst with respect to the PHILSOM system is:

(1) Take a set of input data whose total number of combinations run into the billions (only a few hundred of which are reasonable), (2) write a single unvarying sequence of instructions and (3) without regard to context produce the orderly lists of data that are PHILSOM'S output. Furthermore the analyst must accomplish this in an environment foreign to his (the analyst's) nature.

Keeping this description of a computer in mind let us direct our attention to the PHILSOM system.

The PHILSOM system is quite neatly bisected into two major phases, the file maintenance phase and the output phase. Comparatively few things are done in places other than where they belong. The occasional task that is displaced is done so for economic reasons. The ideal way, rigidly adhered to, can sometimes cause a sharp increase in processing time.

The first two programs in PHILSOM accomplish the file maintenance function. Program "A" validates the input, those transactions that cannot be processed because of a clerical error are prevented from entering the system. Currently only about fifteen errors slip into the system in a month out of approximately 13,000 transactions, a rate

which reflects the high level of care exercised by the members of the PHILSOM Network. Program "B" produces as its primary output a new "Master File," that is, it organizes the data and records it all in one place for month to month storage.

The remaining programs in the system are concerned with selecting, formatting and printing data on the various outputs.

Each printed output may be thought of as a one-to-one mapping of the master file to obtain a specific printed output. The term "mapping" may be unfamiliar to some. It has a mathematical definition, and it is also a concept that is quite useful in programming. Without undue formality, it is the relationship that exists between sets of objects. For example, squaring a number may be thought of as a mapping of one set of numbers into another. Two maps into four, four into sixteen, etc. Now squaring is a regular function which we can memorize or compute. It is, however, simply a special case of the general definition. Another way to think of mapping is to consider the mapping of a number into its symbol or numeral. We think of two objects, of duality, or of "twoness" and we represent it with the symbol for two (2). The symbol (2) has no meaning of its own, but it does have a relationship to the abstract idea of twoness.

In programming, the simultaneous process of code conversion and rearrangement each time a line of printed output is composed may be thought of as a mapping of the master record into a line of presentation output. In PHILSOM, the conversion from internal machine code to normal spelling may be thought of as a mapping. Another form of mapping that is important in programming is the rearrangement or mapping into space that takes place when preparing print lines. For example, the Master Titles List is printed in an order quite different from the way it is recorded on the Philsom master file.

The PHILSOM system has many different outputs, sixteen to be exact. Each of these may be thought of as a separate mapping of the master file into a report. Furthermore, there are variations between users. For example, our desk copy carries a line at the top of each page informing our users that holdings dated before 1900 are kept in storage. Each variation also may be thought of as a mapping. These mappings can be implemented via a computer program.

It would obviously be simple but tedious to write a separate program for every output for each user. This approach would necessitate reading the master file ninety-three times with our present user population and, of course, is not a satisfactory solution.

If we think of the printing requirements in PHILSOM we will find a great deal of overlap. The programming activities for those portions of the printing task which are heavily overlapped need doing only once. All members of the network share in the expense. This is the reason for urging standardization in format. Absolute standardization is unrealistic. Different users have different operational procedures and therefore different requirements. However, we must remember, uniqueness is costly.

The way the PHILSOM system handles the print problem is to pass the master file once and partially format all printed data. The output from this program is three semi-formatted reels of tape. Three other programs complete the task. Each produces several of the PHILSOM outputs, each does that portion of the total task unique to specific users.

We propose to rework portions of the PHILSOM print programs. When we do, we want the programs to be as *modular* as possible. Now modular is a word that is used with some regularity in information processing. The meaning of the term has not always been crystal clear. Modularity always means subdividing a task (program). However, it is my belief that when properly applied to the programming task modularity has a deeper meaning. It means the division of a large task into smaller ones along logical or functional boundries. We have already mentioned the division of large information processing systems along functional boundries. In PHILSOM the file maintenance function is separated from the preparation of presentation output. Within a program further splitting takes place. For example, the reading and writing of data files are usually separated from other processing.

With respect to PHILSOM, splitting the print preparation function into a number of non-overlapping routines is perhaps the most important division. Recall, we are considering the formatting of presentation output as a one-to-one mapping. The selection of each variable from the master file and its subsequent placement in the print line can be considered a *micro-task*. The work necessary to prepare a complete line of output for transmission to the printer therefore consists of a series or a *set* of micro-tasks. Philsom has many rather complicated outputs. This means the number of different print lines or sets of micro-tasks is quite large. The job of getting PHILSOM printed is fortunately not the sum of all printing tasks, but rather their union. When viewed as the union of sets of micro-tasks, we can distinguish a number of different regions. Some of these regions are unique to an individual, some common to all and some regions used by some but not all users. These regions are non-overlapping sub-sets of the full set of micro-tasks and they represent the smallest number of divisions which will be flexible enough to satisfy all users. I shall call them the *atoms* of processing. It is along these lines that the program should be divided, each atom implemented as a program modual. Some of these moduals will be quite large, some very small. I believe the size of the program moduals need not be uniform, but should conform to the atomic structure of the total task.

It is in this direction that the PHILSOM system will evolve. The symmetry of such an organization is esthetically pleasing. The print program reads the master file and looks at each user's needs with respect to the record in processes. The intermediate result will be a list of atoms (possibly none) that are required by a specific user on the record in process. The program will execute the moduals needed and go

on to the next user. When the array of users is exhausted, the program will fetch the next record from the master file and again cycle through the array of users. This organization should be a great help to the co-ordinator of the network; minor changes in any member's requirements can be met by changing only a single atom.

Consider also the orderly streamlined way a new user may be added to the network. The prospective member could be shown an exhibit of all PHILSOM documents. If the prospective member found his needs satisfied by some combination of available atoms, this set of atoms and the user identification could be added to the table, the could program modified to handle a larger user population, and the enrollment would be complete. If the new member required something unique, the programming effort to create the new atom would be borne entirely by the new member. This is the fairest way for veteran members.

To summarize; this form of analysis is a top-down decomposition of the project starting with the grossest functional divisions of the job and continuing down to the most elementary level. Next, the atoms of processing are defined. Atoms are programming units that do not cross functional boundries and are directed toward a homogeneous user population. These atoms will be simple in construction since, by their definition, they do not contain decisions with respect to program control. Finally, program control is made flexible and confined to a separate program modual.

This analysis represents a more formal of approach the programming problem than has been taken in the past. However, these methods are theoretically sound and have been proven in practice.

The current system organization is indeed directed toward many of these same goals. The effect of minor changes over time have blurred some of the original program lines. We hope by formalizing the program design goals and making all future modifications with the program organization clearly in mind to steadily and continually enhance the operational effectiveness of the PHILSOM system.

THE PHILSOM NETWORK: MAINTENANCE AND DESIGN

Millard Johnson

At the Washington University School of Medicine the developmental demands for automation of the library are translated into design specifications by the Research Associate in Machine Methods in a department known as the Machine Project. In this paper I — as Research Associate — hope to show how I work with PHILSOM'S administrators, coordinator and the computer center's systems personnel to maintain PHILSOM in optimum efficiency. I will try to show why maintenance of even a well designed system is a never ending task and give some particulars as to the kind of continuing development that goes into PHILSOM.

I would now like to take a moment to discuss the organization of the Machine Project as the developmental arm for the automation of the Library. I do this because I feel that we are better organized for this than most libraries. In fact, of all the aspects of the PHILSOM system, the developmental organization is the one aspect I can recommend unequivocally in all environments — almost. Many libraries (though this is becoming less true) have no *formal* structure for incorporating new developments. When a new automated project is decided upon they tend to place the system designer under the head of the department in which the system will be used. The next step is to hire a programmer and, if possible, buy a computer. In my opinion this is analogous to building and operating a power plant to provide light for the library stacks. At the Washington University Medical School Library the Research Associate's job is a staff rather than a line position. My job is mainly experimental and developmental. I am not in the chain of command of any department, and have supervisory responsibility only for data preparation. When programming or computing is needed we buy only as much as we need and we are not restricted to a single programmer or computer.

The Machine Project has its own budget and most of its operating funds come from general improvement grants through the Dean of the Medical School. Thus, the budgets of other library departments would not increase if all research were cancelled. The stated goal of the Machine Project is to test new techniques and machines in the medium sized medical library environment. Since PHILSOM has been in operation since 1968 it comes to my attention only for what I will broadly call maintenance which I will discuss in a moment.

Acquaintances often ask "since you are a librarian and you don't check out the books — what do you do?" This question is especially difficult in respect to PHILSOM. Since I supervise no one, make no library-wide decisions, and do very little programming it may appear that I should check out books. But, my main function in PHILSOM, as

I see it, is to act as a system monitor, to try to keep the system functioning optimally in its changing environment. I also act to translate the needs of the librarian into the vocabulary of the analyst/programmer.

This is a good place to point out that anyone who thinks he will design a large scale automated serials control system, program it and forget it is in for a serious shock. The reason that such an approach is naive is that we live in a world of change, change not only in the methods and hardware of computing, but in the expectations and demands of users. Industry-wide figures show that operating systems annually spend between 20% and 40% of the development costs on the maintenance of operating systems. In PHILSOM we are now below that range; neverthless PHILSOM regularly takes 15 to 20% of my time.

PHILSOM maintenance is certainly not the most enjoyable part of my life. I think that most systems people would agree that the most satisfying part of the profession is gathering specifications and working on the design of a new application. The execution of that design is less interesting and the maintenance can be downright drudgery. PHILSOM maintenance would indeed be drudgery, but for the fact that PHILSOM has such a powerful personality.

Mrs. Feagler has described the output of PHILSOM. The computer program itself is really a series of five COBOL programs. These were not the most efficient in the world when they were written, and now that they bear the stamp of at least seven programmers, they are even less so. But, the programs do what they are supposed to. They digest and output over ½ million lines of data each month. This is about 16 cartons or 300 pounds of paper. I feel that PHILSOM's personality is like that of a big sloppy dog's; you can curse it and love it at the same time.

Another point which influences my view of PHILSOM is that PHILSOM and I meet only when someone in the network is dissatisfied with the system. Thus, PHILSOM is a continuing source of both satisfaction and frustration. It is satisfying to be making people more happy with an already good package, but frustrating never to reach that point of perfection where no one wants anything the system does not provide. In my 18 months as Research Associate, there has never been a time when at least one refinement to the system has not been somewhere in the development stream; and what is more, the cue of desired program modifications continues to grow to the point that I now have 8 tasks that at least one person in the network would like to see implemented.

Does this mean that PHILSOM is a poorly designed system? I think not. In fact, I think quite the contrary is true. Basically librarians who use the system are happy with it and when they have gained confidence with it and familiarity with its products, their time is freed and they unleash their imagination to request products the original designers had not envisioned.

Now that I have discussed how the Machine Project is organized to perform maintenance on PHILSOM, I would like to give an idea of the kinds of tasks that are performed and how they come to my attention.

The first and most trivial kind of maintenance is the elimination of design and programming errors. In this case PHILSOM simply does not do what it is supposed to do. About six months ago PHILSOM was cheerfully chugging along on its monthly run when it suddenly stopped. Working day and night for two days we found that when the subscription to a title which was exactly 70 characters long, the 69th character of which was blank, was encountered, the program aborted. This is an example of a latent program bug which no reasonable amount of testing could be expected to find. It is possible, I would say even probable, that in a program the size and complexity of PHILSOM other such bugs exist; though it may take another 7 years to find the next one. Another example is to be found on our recent work on fiscal reports. In this case, our bible, *New PHILSOM Documentation 2nd edition*, which is here for your examination, said what fiscal data PHILSOM would produce. However, the program logic and the documentation did not agree. Here we simply changed the program to produce the output specified in the documentation.

When the need for recovery from design and programming errors occurs, time is usually critical. Since we cannot hold up PHILSOM production for the usual estimate, evaluation and job authorization, I will usually authorize work on these problems over the telephone with only brief consultation with the librarian and the PHILSOM coordinator.

The second kind of work PHILSOM demands is development to bring the system in line with the changing demands of its users. I have come to the conclusion that the user is insatiable. He always wants more than the system can give. Ask the librarian everything he could possibly want from a serials system—program all these features and before the ink is dry on the first output he will have thought of a new feature he would really like to see implemented. This faculty of the human mind is the foundation of my livelihood. I am faced with the paradox of the clinical physician. I want all my systems to remain vital, but if they do for long, I will be unemployed. Fortunately or unfortunately, PHILSOM users have never let me down. They are always ready with a suggestion for improvement. When they receive more than one copy of a journal they would like to have the set number appear on their binding slip. They would like to be able to delete a single issue from their holdings statement without resubmitting full holdings information. They would also like to have each journal's invoice number appear on the librarian's work copy as well as fiscal reports. These are just a few examples of the numerous changes PHILSOM's users would like to see.

I usually become aware of these needs through Mrs. Feagler. The local librarian will ask her if a change is possible. I then screen the

requests into those that are impossible in the present system, those that are possible but of long term nature, and those of local interest. PHILSOM administrators (this year Dr. Brodman and Mr. Schmidt) with the consultation of Mrs. Feagler and myself, then set priorities. I then write work orders to computer center programmers and when tests prove that specifications are met, Mrs. Feagler will then accept the work. If the change is of local interest only, I will act as a mediator between the individual library and the computer center. In this case I draw specifications satisfactory to that library, then get an estimate from the computer center. If the estimate is satisfactory, the work is done with the individual library paying for features used only by itself.

I would like to point out to people thinking of designing for networking that the dominant theme of user suggested changes is toward local individualization of output. The user does not much care how the data is stored or manipulated, but he is extremely interested in exactly what data appears where on his output. He may recognize the necessity for standardization of input format and bibliographic authority, but he demands control, without intervention, of his own data.

The final catagory of my work is best described as obsolescence maintenance—obsolescence of hardware, and software conventions. I think the most dramatic changes in the PHILSOM system that we will see this year are in this category. Mr. Falvey has discussed the modular programming concepts now being employed in PHILSOM. We started this project with the modest goal of being able to process serials for more than ten libraries but we have taken the opportunity to rewrite large segments of the program using the modular technique. In the future each library will have its print module. This valuable technique was not in common usage in 1968, but with it local libraries may specify receiving output as magnetic tape or COM microform, which are themselves options not widely available many years ago.

Modular programming is only one example of evolving technique but I would like to point out that systems designers invariably constrain their designs to available technology. In PHILSOM for example the limitation of the 80 column tab card is everywhere evident. But in as dynamic an environment as modern-day computers, even the best systems are doomed to a short life expectancy. Thus, even though I consider PHILSOM one of the most valuable and cost effective systems available at this time, and we are constantly working on the system to keep it up-to-date, I expect PHILSOM to be completely obsolete by 1976. To that end I am gathering specifications for PHILSOM's successor, PHILSOM 3, and I am considering such parameters as MARC serials format, ISSN and on-line remote processing.

In this paper I have presented PHILSOM as a problem that needs attention. This is the basis of my contact with all of the library's production programs. But PHILSOM is in fact a highly successful system. I believe the cruelest test of any system is to offer it for sale on the open market and this is where PHILSOM has proven itself. It is the

primary serials control for seven major medical libraries and another PHILSOM center is now being established by the Medical Library Center of New York. Some of the reasons for this success have been voiced by the other members of this panel but I think that one of the chief attributes of the system is that it is dynamic. Almost everyone in the network would like to see at least one aspect of the system changed but where PHILSOM differs from some other computer-based systems is that it has built into its system concept a mechanism for feedback, evaluation and change.

THE PHILSOM NETWORK: A USER LIBRARY VIEWPOINT

Dean Schmidt

At the Medical Library of the University of Missouri-Columbia, we have been involved with PHILSOM since March 1970. Up to that time we had closely reviewed our method of serial record keeping, were not pleased with it, but were not able to do anything about it. Our method was to check-in currently received titles on a kardex which was located at our Circulation Desk, record bound volumes in a shelf list which was located in a work room. We tried to maintain a mimeograph list of all titles available in the library—and I do mean tried. Our periodical situation was further complicated by the fact that we are a branch library in a centralized system and therefore much of the activity involving serials has to be done in or through that main library. For example, our catalog cards for serials all have LC entries and call numbers, yet we use and always have used direct titles for shelving and for circulation.

We realized we were not satisfied with the way we were maintaining our serial records, so we began looking around for a system in which we could have the type of records we wanted, but also we wanted a system in which we would be able to take over certain functions that were being accomplished at our main library. Now that we are in PHILSOM, we have records that we like, but have not yet become independent of our main library in all aspects of serials management.

Before deciding on a method of serials management we asked ourselves what type of serial records did we really want. We knew we wanted a complete list of all titles, current and dead. We wanted complete up-to-date holding statements, including both bound volumes and unbound issues, we wanted lists that could be available in multiple locations, and easily reproduced. We also wanted better control of binding and we wanted information on whether an item was received as a gift or on subscription. All this sort of data was only available at the main library. We also felt that we needed to use direct titles, as they are used in *Index Medicus* because we felt that any such standardization or consistency that we could employ would be an aid to our users.

It was about this time that we began thinking about an automated system versus a different manual system. Our University Library had years of experience with automation, although not with serial records, and we had long ago learned *the hard way* that automation did not mean less expense or less staff so we had to ask whether or not we could afford either added personnel for a better manual system or could we afford an automated system as well as the added personnel? This was a hard question to answer, particularly since our costs could not be documented. I also asked the question, "what kind of a system would be suitable and economical for us at the present but still would

be a suitable system for handling serial records in five or ten years when, hopefully, the number of titles that we would hold would have increased by an appreciable number." I became convinced that instead of a more encompassing manual record, some sort of automated system would be more desirable. I had been for some years aware of PHILSOM as it was being used at Washington University. Also I did not have the staff, the time or the money to develop a unique system for our library, nor did I think it necessary that we devise a unique system that could take care of all the peculiarities which may have found its way into our serial management, or which could be imagined as an aid to our staff and patrons. Since the capabilities of PHILSOM were known to me, since it had developed to a point where additional libraries could be added, and because there was nothing similar the decision was made to enter into an agreement with Washington University.

Next we had to determine how far into PHILSOM did we wish to go. We knew we wanted to add all titles, dead or current, but we didn't know if we should enter current titles first and add all others at a later date. We had to decide whether or not we wanted to enter all data, such as bindery and fiscal. But along with these questions, we had to ask who was going to be responsible for the continuity of the system within our library.

Because of the small staff at our library and because of turnover of the serials staff at that time, I took an active part in entering into the system. Three months later, we started to get anticipation cards and had a printed PHILSOM, but we continued to check-in journals in the old manual fashion. When the new serials librarian arrived, we almost immediately came to St. Louis for her training and introduction to PHILSOM. Then we updated our records for the three months since data was originally supplied, and began checking in all new receipts through PHILSOM. We did not run a dual system, except for those titles that were not yet recorded in the automated system, and those were entered immediately.

We fortunately continue to have the same serials librarian and she has done much to promote the acceptance of PHILSOM within our library. Of all the attributes a librarian may bring to this sort of a position, I feel that a sound introduction to computers and automated systems, which enables one to understand the logic and capabilities of a system like PHILSOM is of the greatest value.

In order to better explain how PHILSOM is used at our library, I'll give you a more complete description of how we entered into it. At the time we started using PHILSOM, the Medical Library was receiving about 1500 current periodical titles. We decided to enter all current and dead titles at the same time, with the exception of some annual reports and a few technical reports of various governmental agencies. Since we were one of the first libraries to enter the PHILSOM network, we found that we had many new titles to add and therefore we had to submit bibliographic data as well as holdings, but fortunately we added all of

those in the format of UCMP, if possible. Also on our campus is a Veterinary Medical Library which receives about 400 current titles. I am administratively reponsible for the Veterinary Medical Library and they are very heavy users of our collection. Also their holdings often compliment our collection in that it duplicates some of the heaviest used medical periodicals. It also has some titles we would own if the Veterinary Medical Library were not available to us. The periodical collections of these two libraries constituted our basic input into PHILSOM, but soon after joining the network, we added and continue to add many monographic serials for which we never did have adequate records since these items were received and processed through our main library. Two years after entering into PHILSOM a Veterans Administration hospital opened across the street from the Medical Center. As soon as its new librarian arrived, I talked to her about the possibility of including their periodicals in PHILSOM. Our administrations had instructed us to cooperate to the utmost. As a matter of fact, the situation was almost ideal as most of the professional staff of the VA Hospital have joint appointments in the Medical Center and our students, both medical and nursing, and the residents and interns rotate between the two facilities. Therefore, it was felt that one type of periodical holding record would be easier for the users as well as giving them a better idea of exactly what medical periodicals were available. The titles in the VA Library are the heaviest used medical periodicals and augment our collection.

At the present time there are about 2350 current sets and 1800 dead sets, representing about 3400 titles, recorded in our PHILSOM printout, which includes and it is a small network the holdings of the major health science libraries in Columbia. Actually there is only one other medical collection and that is at the State's Cancer Research Hospital. We would perhaps include their holdings if PHILSOM developed to the point where more than four sets of each cumulation can be produced. We use all four sets now because the Medical Library requires two. Each of the smaller libraries report to our serials librarian, who in turn advises them, and submits the data, corrections, receipt cards, etc. to Washington University. Since the University Library pays for PHILSOM, it includes the expenses for the Veterinary Medical Library, but we do charge the VA Hospital on the basis of the number of titles recorded for them.

PHILSOM has been extremely well received by the Medical librarians in our area largely because of the interdependent nature of the three libraries involved. The greatest benefit to the staff and users is being able to have complete lists of holdings in several locations. These provide not only holdings, but accurate, documented bibliographic data with adequate cross references, notes, etc. Even though this bibliographic data is rather rigidly controlled, the system does allow for some flexibility as to locations, special handling or other special notes that any individual library may desire. At first the staff did not use

PHILSOM as often as they should have, but the serials librarian and I usually answered their questions concerning serials by asking if they checked PHILSOM. After one has the staff using PHILSOM, one must be sure that they can read the records properly, and this is sometimes more difficult than one would imagine. The staff is now trained to report errors and strange looking things to the serials librarian so corrections can be made. One complaint has been that the records do not show whether a volume is bound or not. Having the periodical shelf list near by provides an answer to that question.

We distribute copies of PHILSOM to other libraries which do not participate in the system, for instance a life science research library on campus, and the Medical School Library at the Kansas City campus.

The patrons use PHILSOM frequently and for the most part interpret it well. Primarily they like it because copies are available on each of the stack levels. We have had up to now no requests from individual faculty members or any of the teaching departments for copies of the lists.

In addition to the serials holdings list we receive monthly a number of other outputs. First of all, there are the anticipation cards, usually about 2000 of them, for all issues scheduled for publication during the next month. Since these are arranged alphabetically, it is necessary to sort out the cards for the other two libraries. Those for the Medical Library must then be interfiled with those remaining from previous months. This file has between 4000 and 6000 cards in it at all times.

The claim lists, another output, has been coded so that a separate list is provided for each of the libraries. It is checked against new receipts and in general we find that about two-thirds of the items listed have been received since the run, or have already been claimed. At this time we do not mail copies of them as claim letters, but if possible we hope to do so at some later date.

The bind slips are used internally but at the present time are not acceptable to the binder used by the University of Missouri. However, after our initial entry into PHILSOM, we did code in binding frequency, information from the title page and index, information as to whether we bind in ads or not, as well as the title code and color code used by our binder. We hope that soon we will be able to have the bind slip formated so as to be acceptable to him. We have devised a system utilizing the bind slips to see that the Veterinary Medical Library and the Medical Library do not send the same volumes to the bindery at the same time.

The diagnostic list is used primarily to correct errors that we have submitted on receipt cards as well as to keep us informed of the many titles for which we have received no issues for some time. We check this against current receipts, as well as against the union list which is received four times a year and the monthly input lists. This informs us whether another library has received the item or not, and therefore guides us in deciding to claim.

The union list is also of value to the interlibrary loan and acquisitions departments. In interlibrary loan we use it two ways. We can check to see if other libraries have received an issue which we do not have, but suspect may have been published. Also we may be able to locate a library where the title is held. In acquisitions it helps us to decide whether we should purchase a title or not based on the availability in other libraries in our region.

Subject, language and location lists are requested as desired, but we find that this does not have to be done very frequently. The subject list appears to be of the greatest value.

Since our fiscal affairs are handled by our main university library, we do not use that aspect of PHILSOM, but we may at some later date. However, as an aid in claiming we have entered the standing order number, and the source of each subscription.

In addition to these aspects of PHILSOM, we have made additions or modifications for use within our library. Early in the game, we found that it was necessary to keep punch cards for all issues without anticipation cards, this is in contrast to submitting the data to Washington University and having them key punch it for the run. We soon learned to extend this to punching anticipation cards for items whose frequency is so irregular that it was impossible to code correctly. For example, *Biochimica et Biophysica Acta* which will publish 41 volumes in 1973 with issues from seven different volumes being published in January. We take the list that appears in the first issue of the year and key punch cards for the entire year.

Our serials librarian devised a method for putting notes of various sorts into our file of anticipation cards. For example, we receive many gift issues which we do not keep in the library. As an aid to our check-in clerk, we make up a number, not used in PHILSOM, punch it into a card and then write the title and instructions on the card.

Presently we are developing an on-line circulation system for our library. We are adapting a system that is being used off-line by our main university library. This uses call numbers as access, but since we use direct titles for serials, we are using the PHILSOM number instead of the call number and PHILSOM type abbreviations as our standard.

Another use of PHILSOM that we hope to implement soon is to add all titles which are indexed in *Index Medicus*, but located on our campus in libraries other than the Medical or Veterinary Medical Library. We will merely list the title with a note indicating title available in, for example, the Science Library.

Three years of association with PHILSOM has taught us a great deal. We have learned to cooperate with other libraries. We have learned a great deal about serials management and something about automated systems. We have learned that it takes a lot of effort to achieve good results, but that the effort and expense are worth it in terms of the improved services that we can provide to our users. I'm sure that added effort and imagination will produce better results and further improved services in the future.

CASE STUDY OF THE COMPUTER ASSISTED SERIALS SYSTEM AT THE UNIVERSITY OF CALIFORNIA, SAN DIEGO

by Don L. Bosseau

I. Introduction

II. The Original System

    A. Development

    B. Description

        1. Organization and policies
        2. Definitions
        3. Operations

    C. Problems

III. Transition

IV. The New System

    A. Design considerations

    B. Description

V. Review

    A. Staffing and Costs

    B. Commentary

I. INTRODUCTION

In a sort of oral history format, you are going to hear about one of the oldest and largest continuously operating serials systems making use of computer processing capabilities. I say oldest because the system started as a project in 1961, began limited operation in 1962 and has been operating ever since. In terms of the size of the operation, the system grew from an initial number of around 1500 records that it was processing in 1963 to 31,000 records at the present time (See Figure 1). Of the 31,000 records, 24,232 are serial titles, and the rest are cross-references. To give you an idea of the rapid growth that the system accommodated, the number of active titles grew in that same period from around 700 to nearly 14,000 titles by 1973.

Characteristic	1962	1963	1964	1965	1966	1967	1968	1969	1973
Number of volumes in University Library System ...	67,000	111,000	180,000	260,000	337,000	420,000	520,000	630,000	1,000,000
Total number of entries in serials system	700	1,500	3,000	7,916	11,194	13,576	20,467 (incl 1937 x-refs)	22,400 (incl 2700 x-refs)	30,810 (incl 6578 x-refs)
Number of active titles in serials system	"	"	"	5,815	7,677	9,054	11,555	12,200	13,742
Computer costs for monthly update		$127.00					$676.00	$800.00	$900.00
Paper costs (including binding, deleaving, etc.		$ 21.00					$160.00	$400.00	$800.00
Number of master-lists required	1	1	1	5	10	15	12	11	12
Landmarks: Pilot project .... Operation of initial system and programming of improved version .. Parallel records dropped Original system operation Design and programming new system .... New system	↑		↑			↑	↑	↑	↑

Figure 1. Brief Chronology of the UCSD Serials System

Now for those of you, or anyone for that matter who is dubious about the reliability of storing such detailed records on mag tape, especially records which are internally changed and updated routinely, then please take note of the fact that there were never any parallel records except for a brief period during the first year's operation. The only records of holdings have been stored on magnetic tape and this master file has been updated every month since 1964 without fail. Needless to say, the system has survived, perhaps I should say "outlived," several computers, turnover in personnel, turnover in programmers and systems staff, and has served the student body and faculty that has grown from less than 1,000 to nearly 10,000 on campus.

The UC San Diego Serials System has indeed been flexible in its ability to accommodate the routine changes that must occur in any serials operation. At the same time, regimentation of many of the manual procedures often associated with a computer assisted operation such as this has actually been advantageous to librarians and users alike. This results from the fact that all records are uniform and have been maintained with consistency seldom found in a purely manual system.

To give you some perspective as to what I'll be talking about, I'd like to briefly characterize the system by explaining the mode of operation, and the products it provides. The system is now and always has been a batch operation, involving card input, magnetic tape storage and computer manipulation of serials data, which after the update process is then output onto tapes that are printed to provide the various holdings lists, transaction or arrivals list, binding lists, etc. Central to the system's design philosophy are two basic concepts: 1) The holdings records are created by the automatic cumulation of receipt data; and 2) prediction of expected arrivals is algorithmically generated for as many serials as possible (this allows for assisting in claiming).

Perhaps the best way to relate the events which have occurred in this system over the past 10 or 11 years would be to tell you about the development period and the types of considerations that were taken into account, and to explain how the original system ran for the first four or five years. Then we'll explore the types of problems confronted and some of the reasoning that went into the latest version of the system which is the one that has been operating the last few years. (I started to say final design instead of latest version, but my experience has shown me that the existing system is, as the next system will also be, an interim system by definition.) Obviously I'm going to have to skip over some details, but where the details are pertinent, I might belabor them a little, so that you do get an understanding of just what was really going on at that point in time.

II. THE ORIGINAL SYSTEM
A. **Development:**
The UCSD computer assisted serials operation had a rather

conventional beginning, but had a somewhat unique result among early library automation efforts (circa 1961) in that it is one of the few that is still running.

In the summer of 1961 a series of informal discussions between Melvin Voigt, University Librarian, and the director of the campus computer center led to the idea of automating the control of serials in the library. Serials were decided upon at the time for several reasons including: serials processing is costly, the resulting records of traditional methods were difficult to use and were not generally accessible to the users through the card catalog, (serials are the most important library materials in the sciences, graduate science curricula constituted the only UCSD academic programs at the time), and the repetitive nature of successive updatings of serial records was thought to provide an appropriate application of mechanization.[1] Since the University Library was in its beginning stages of developing its collection, its relative small size simplified some of the problems associated with this type of project. In addition, it was felt that the problems of rapid expansion which the library would undergo in the ensuing years could possibly be simplified through the use of computer applications. Dynamic growth would also prove to be a strong test for the system.

A modest proposal by today's standards for assistance with the project resulted in a grant of $10,000 from the office of former President Clark Kerr of the University of California. This grant permitted work to begin in November of 1961.

The initial phase took care of the preliminaries. Scattered records were consolidated into a central serials file, a step which is an achievement with or without the computer (as some librarians will attest to!). Also, the components of the serial record were identified and analyzed with respect to requirements of putting them into machine readable form. These included location (i.e., where each title is to be shelved), call number, title, complete holdings statement and inclusive year dates, date (month and year) of latest issue received, status (subscription, gift or exchange), fund, source, and expiration of subscription date. Finally, the types of output desired were specified. The output was to consist of the following items:

1. Complete holdings lists of all serials.
2. Lists of current receipts of periodicals by location.
3. Bindery lists of all serials received unbound.
4. Claims lists for all serials.
5. Non-receipt lists for all serials.
6. Expiration of subscription lists for all purchased serials.

The basic input ground rule was that "checking-in" of serials was to be a simple procedure that would update the master files.

To a great extent the actual design and development stages were closely tied to the initial analysis since the elements of input and output were adjusted through feedback from serials personnel and from the programmer; i.e., as programs were being written, additional data

were recognized as being essential to satisfy the objectives. This information was constantly reviewed and the corrections were incorporated into the record gathering as well as the program designs. The result was the addition of more data to the serial record components noted earlier, including a unique serial identification number, class, number of issues per volume, number of issues per year, regularity of appearance, day of the month of the last issue received for weekly and biweekly serials, number of last issue for continuous issue numbers, and a mnemonic title.

In retrospect the system appears to actually have developed by a process of evolution in lieu of following a formal set of design specifications. Thus, the design was determined by actual needs as they were recognized. In 1961 when all of this started, there was no place to turn for help except to converse with colleagues and to transcribe experience with conventional serials operations into computer-programmable concepts. The emphasis was placed on those areas which promised improved cost effectiveness and service.

The original computer program was written in FORTRAN 60 language for the CDC 1604 computer. Initial testing began upon completion of the computer programs. For the purpose of testing, a sample of 100 intermediate serials records was prepared, key-punched on IBM cards, and put on magnetic tape. A set of sample records was then processed by the computer programs. When the programs were shown to work, procedures were designed for the Serials Department staff to maintain, check-in, and update a larger number of serial titles. For this operational phase, it was decided to include all of the titles shelved on the current serial shelves in two reading rooms. Accordingly, 712 intermediate serial records were prepared and transferred to the master file on magnetic tape.

The next distinct phase of the serials project began later in the summer of 1962 with a grant of $13,600 from the Council on Library Resources. A new program was being written in FORTRAN 62 with an influx of subroutines in assembly language. The latter were being used to improve running efficiency on the computer. This new program which is the basis of the original system became operational in April of 1964. During its development, more serial titles were added to the old system, increasing the number from about 700 in July 1962 to 1500 in June 1963. At that time it was decided to hold off putting any new titles into the test system since the new version would soon be ready. Operation of the pilot system continued through April of 1964.

During the period of 1962-63, the serials clerks were noting shortcomings of the old system and making suggestions for changes and new features. The prime improvements to be incorporated were simplification of corrections (file maintenance) and bindery information input.

Of the six output objectives listed earlier, the first system had achieved the first two which provided complete holdings lists of all

serials and daily receipt lists by location (branch library). The refined program produced lists and cards for serials with completed but unbound volumes. These lists, known as bindery lists, served as aids for pulling materials from the shelves which were ready for binding. The bindery cards served as the input to the computer program which caused the appropriate completed and unbound volumes (e.g., U16) to become bound volumes (e.g., B16) in the holdings statements. The claims lists, non-receipt lists and expired subscriptions lists were never implemented.

Figure 1 contains a chart indicating some important events in the system's lifetime, along with its chronological growth. Figures 2a, 2b and 2c are simplified flowcharts of the basic processes involved in the system.

B. **Description:**

1. Organization and Policies (1964-1969):

The Central Serials Department performs cataloging and ordering of serials for the Central University Library, the Science and Engineering Library, the Scripps Institution of Oceanography Library, and the Cluster (undergraduate) Library. The Biomedical Library, using the National Library of Medicine classification system, does its own ordering and cataloging. The Central Serials Department receives and checks-in, and claims overdue issues for the serials of all of the campus libraries (in the new system the Biomedical Library checks-in its own journals). The individual libraries handle bindery preparation, normally assisted by computer produced lists.

The Central Serials Department had a staff of 3 catalogers with 4 check-in personnel who were supervised by a library assistant in charge of the computer aspects of serials. He in turn had an assistant. These were the only personnel directly connected with the computer end of the serials processing.

Daily items such as newspapers are not included in the scope of the serials system. Also, un-numbered monographic series and publishers series and most government documents are in general excluded.

Only main entries are filed into the card catalog for serials and, of course, no holdings are given. The cataloging performed does not give subject headings but does include information statements, i.e., notes on title changes, etc.

2. Definitions:

Since the original system[2] about the be described used computer programs containing many algorithms to predict arrivals and perform other operations, there are some basic concepts with which one needs to become familiar.

Serials fall into either active or inactive status categories. The computer programs cannot automatically update the inactive titles, producing expected arrivals and bindery cards only for the actives. Changes in holdings of inactives are generally entered as a correction type of data input. Active title holdings are updated by submitting the

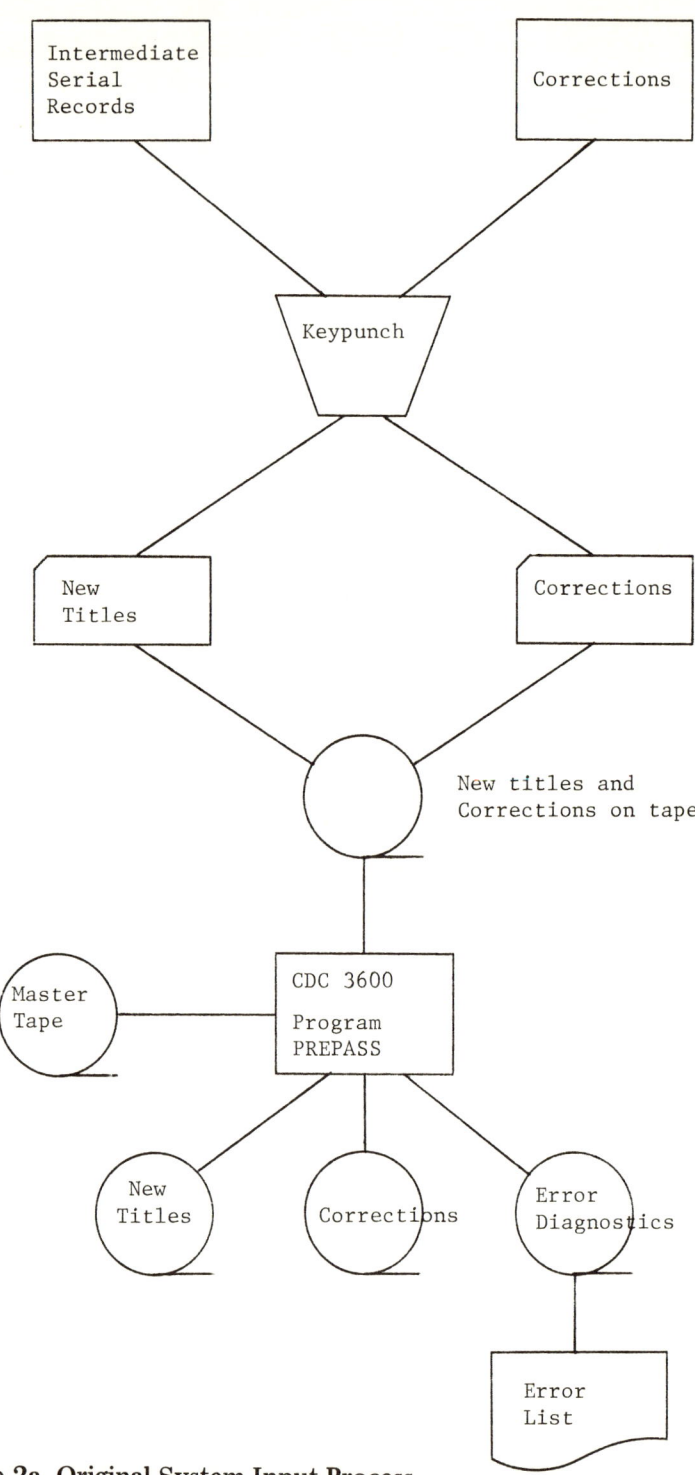

Figure 2a. Original System Input Process

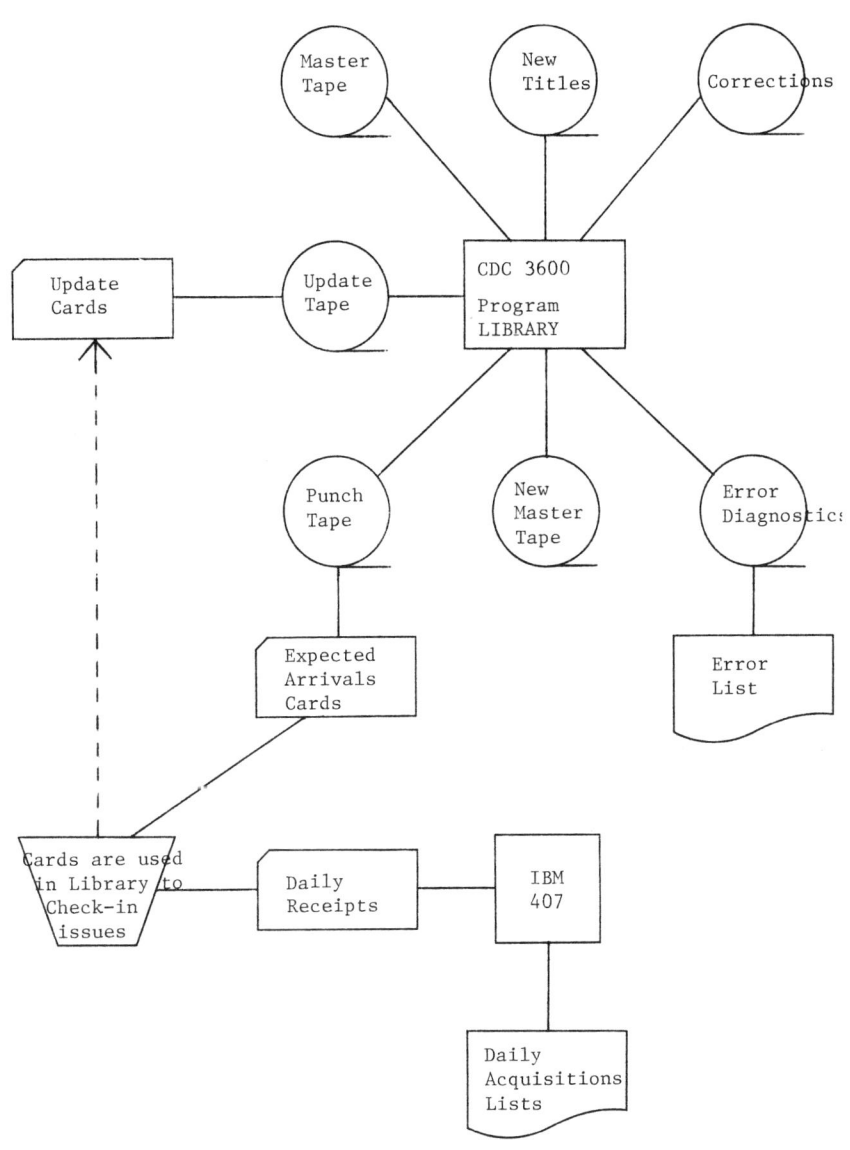

Figure 2b. Original System — Master File Manipulation

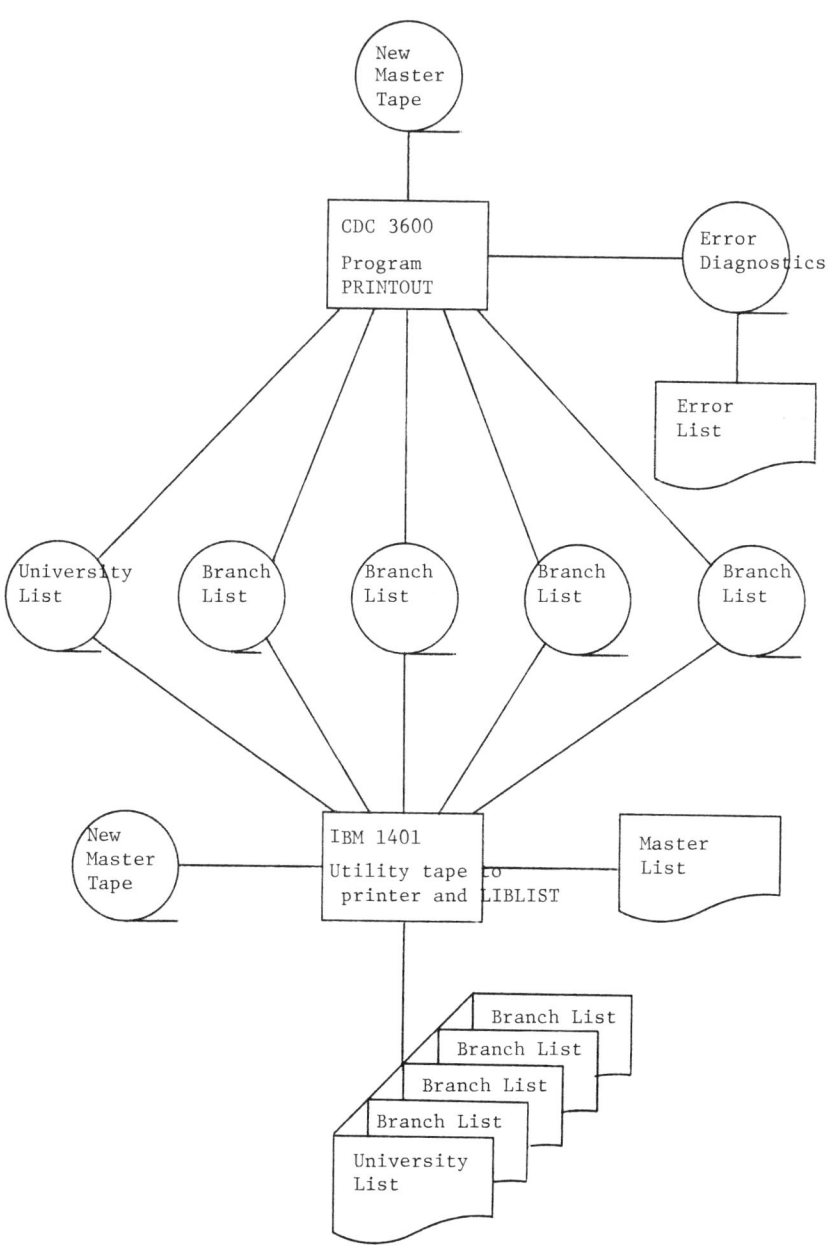

Figure 2c. Original System — Printout

expected arrivals cards. When back periodical orders arrive, the holding are brought up to date by keypunching a new complete holding statement for each title affected and submitting a correction type o input (i.e., file maintenance). This is true of active or inactive titles.

Another pertinent concept concerns the definition of "regularity." A regular journal under the original program's definition was one whic had an equal time interval between issues such as a weekly, monthly, o quarterly publication. The program treated all others not fitting thi simplified definition as irregulars whose arrival could not be predicted Expected arrival cards were produced for regulars only when an issue o issues were expected within the month. Those items which wer irregular did not fit into the prediction mechanism; therefore, the were handled in the following manner. When an issue of an irregula classed serial arrived, an expected arrivals card was pulled an submitted at update time. The program automatically produced a car for the next logical issue to arrive in sequence for that serial. That is i Volume 6, No. 5 was checked in, a card for Volume 6, No. 6 wa produced next. The problem here is that in order to be ready t check-in an irregular you must always have the cards waiting. Thus, th irregular serials caused the expected arrivals file to be cluttered wit cards representing issues which may not arrive for a number of months Also, since any automatic claiming can only be done for regulars, it i more important than ever to have as comprehensive a definition o regular as possible. A statistical study of the master file in 1968 showe 42% of the active titles fell within that old definition of regulars, an another 30% could probably be encompassed by use of a calendar tha I'll explain later. The 30% of serial titles just noted consisted of serial with definite publication schedules but unequal time intervals betweer some or all of the issues; e.g., a journal published monthly except fo June-July and August-September combined issues is certainly a predictable as a straight monthly.

Terminology involving the update cards should also be clarified The terms update cards and expected arrivals cards mean the same thin and are used rather loosely. At the first of the month they were callec the expected arrivals cards. By the time they got pulled to update a journal's holdings, they were more commonly referred to as update cards.

3. Operations:

When a new title enters the system it goes through the process o searching and establishment of proper serial entry before being cataloged. If it is to be an active title or subscription, a standing order gift, or exchange, an interim record is put into a manual file to awai arrival of a first issue to be cataloged.

At the time of cataloging, the Intermediate Serials Records, which is the sample in Figure 3a, is filled out by the cataloger. Spaces 1 through 40 are reserved for fixed-field information. Spaces 41 througl 480 are for variable fields. Figure 3b summarizes the data accomodated

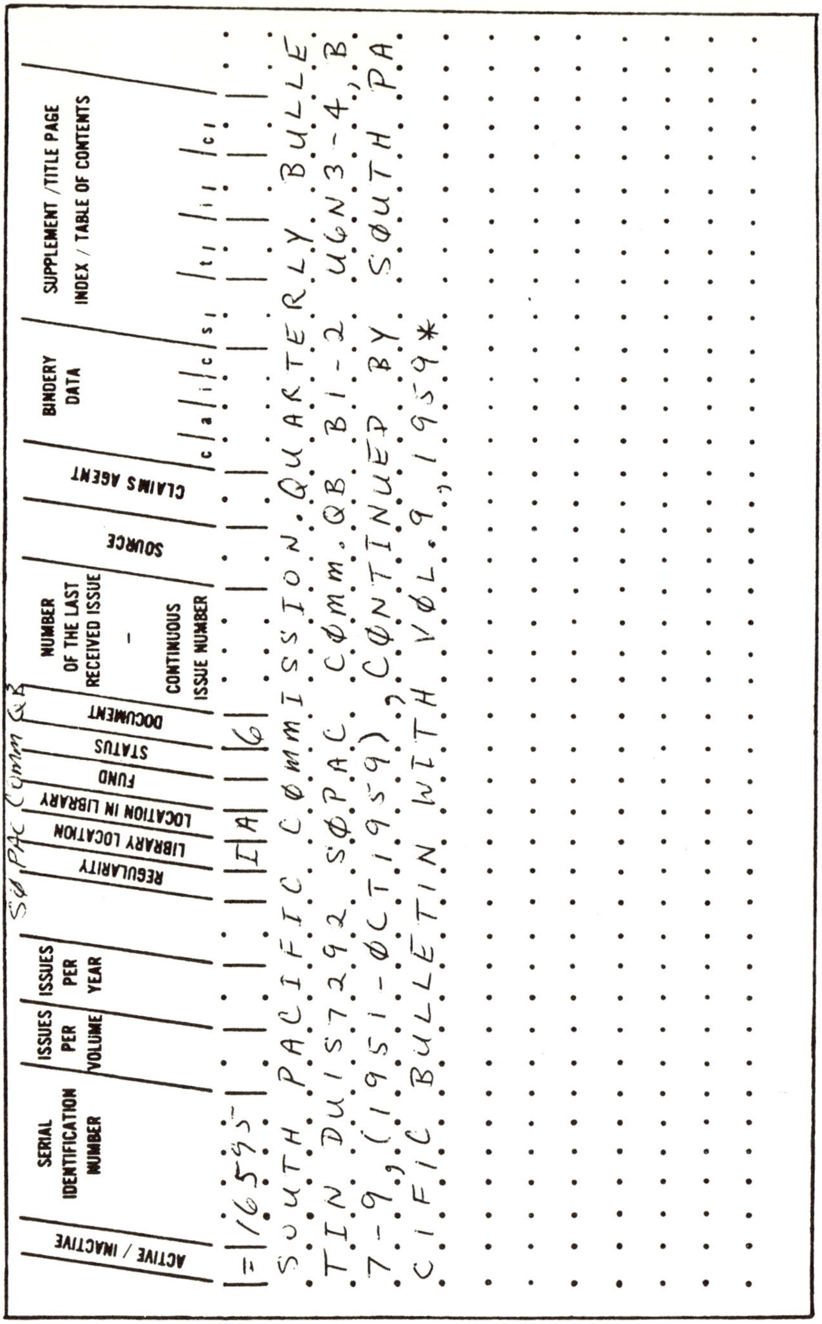

Figure 3a. Intermediate Serials Record

Columns	Information or code(s)
1	Active or inactive title
2 - 6	Identification number
7 - 8	No. of issues per volume
9 - 10	No. of issues per year
11 - 12	Not used at present
13	Regularity or publication pattern
14	Library
15	Shelving location within library
16	Fund
17	Status (i.e., subscription, gift, exchange STO, etc.)
18	Serial or government document
19 - 22	No. of the last received issue
23 - 24	Source (code for the name of vendor, publisher, firm, etc.)
25 - 26	Claims agent (usually same as source)
27	Color of binding
28	Advertisements' treatment (bound in, discard, etc.)
29	Bindingposition of the index
30	Issue covers' treatment
31 - 38	Coding for predicting the arrival of title pages, indexes, and table of content pages; and for the recording of supplements
39 - 40	Not used

Variable Field Data

Field Delimiter	Data
Beginning in 41	Title
$	Call number
$	Formerly mnemonic title (used in the original system)
$	Holdings statement
/	Information notes (title changes, history, etc.)
* (End of record)	

Figure 3b. Fixed Field Information

and the record format used. The 480 space maximum of the pilot system was retained. Experience had shown that few titles exceeded this limit. Those which did invariably had extremely scattered holdings which hopefully would eventually be filled in. In these over-limit cases, as many unit records are made as necessary, with only the latest or current record active. Within the variable field data group was the mnemonic title which had an upper limit of 24 spaces and was the only one in the variable field part of the record with such a limitation. The reason for this was the mnemonic title appeared on the update card (original system only) where all of the necessary information was restricted to 80 spaces. It was essential in the original system that the title abbreviations be easily recognizable, necessitating highly mnemonic symbols. The mnemonic abbreviation was made up locally, and quickly; and was designed to eliminate any look-up.

Records for see references and added entries were treated similarly with the exception that unnecessary information (e.g., no holdings statements) was simply not entered.

Corrections. Under these programs it was possible to make corrections to any space(s) in the fixed field and to any of the variable fields without keypunching the whole record. It was also possible to delete the entire master record or substitute an entire master record. This was a great improvement over the original pilot system of corrections in which the entire record had to be re-written and punched. Entering of newly acquired back volumes or sets of serials, changes in publication appearance or pattern of the serial, transfer of titles to other libraries, changes in location within the libraries, and call number and title are samples of corrections which must be made. Thus, most actions that were called corrections were really file maintenance actions; errors found in the records represented less than 1% of the number of corrections usually submitted. Of course, this doesn't mean there weren't other errors which should be corrected — they just hadn't been caught. Additions, corrections, and updates were the three categories of input at the regular monthly updating time.

Updating. Once a serial record has been incorporated into the master tape, the system will produce pre-punched update cards for all the regular expected issues which will arrive during the next month. These cards were manually interfiled into the expected arrivals file by title.

For irregular serials, the first update card is produced when the serial record is first put on tape. Thereafter, update cards are produced whenever a card for the last issue is returned to the system. For irregular journals that appear more than once a month, the system produced the requisite number of cards per month. Throughout the operation of the old system it was definitely established that the monthly cycle was the optimum time for updating, considering the present growth stage of the library and the size of the serial collection. If corrections, keypunching and additions of new titles were carried out

regularly throughout the month, the workload at update time in these areas was nominal and an update operation could be prepared and accomplished within 1 or 2 days.

The update, or arrivals file card is shown in Figure 4. The various features of the card will be discussed and related to their intended function.

Space 1 was left blank.

Spaces 2 through 6 contained the serial identification number. This number linked the update card to its serial record at the updating procedure. Every record, added entry or see reference, whether the serial is active or inactive, is assigned a unique number, used for retrieval and linkage activities.

Spaces 7 through 31 were reserved for the mnemonic title and copy number, if present. These 25 spaces limit the size of the mnemonic title to 24 spaces to allow for copy number inclusion.

Spaces 32-33 were used for the claim agent code.

Space 34 was a blank.

Spaces 35-60 were reserved for the volume number, issue number, part number, and date or any combinations that were pertinent. These 26 spaces accomodated this information for any title in the system.

Spaces 61-78 were for the call number. The 18 spaces reserved for this item handled any UCSD call number.

Space 79 was reserved for the code letter indicating where the current issue was shelved within the library (or also used for special routing instructions).

With the update card being as self-sufficient as possible, the serials clerk checking in arrived serials was able to process the serial without reference to other records. Once the proper update card was found in the arrivals file, the serials issue was stamped with the proper ownership or location symbol, date, and call number.

Issues with special handling instructions were segregated and distributed later. As the serials for the various libraries or collections were checked in, they were kept in separate piles for shipment to the proper location. The corresponding update cards were similarly segregated. These cards formed the input for the daily receipts lists. At the end of the serial check-in cycle, the cards were alphabetized and taken to the Computer Center for listing. Lists and serials were then sent together to the various libraries.

The listings obtained were used as invoice sheets at their destination and as daily receipt lists which could be posted with the monthly printout, thereby serving as a supplement.

After the daily lists were made, the cards were returned and stored for use in the month's end update. They also were used to provide weekly cumulative listings during the month. Such listings reduced the number of lists necessary to check to determine if a given recent issue of a serial had been received in the library. By merging the weekly lists, further reductions were made. Only the mnemonic title showed on

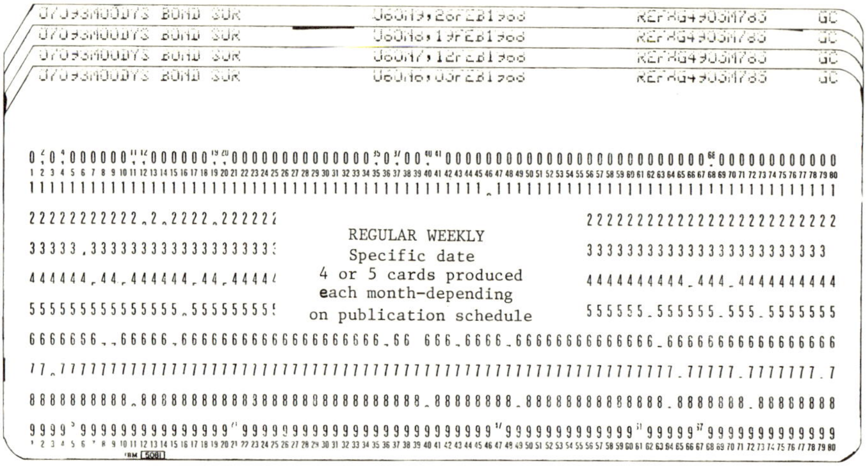

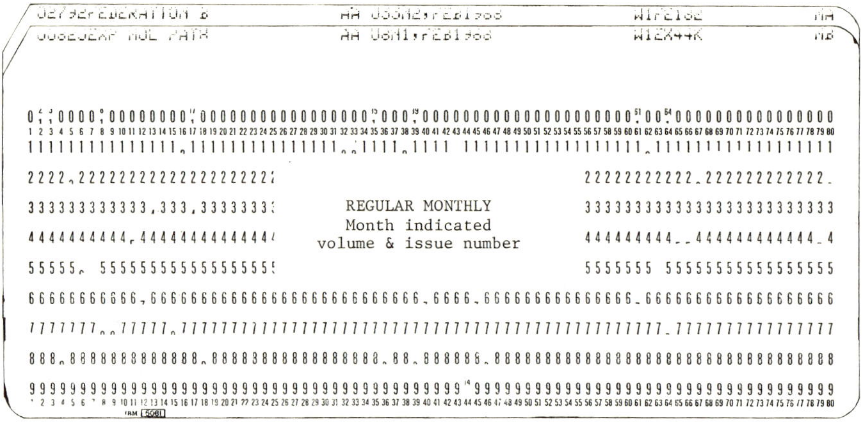

Figure 4. Sample Expected Arrival Cards

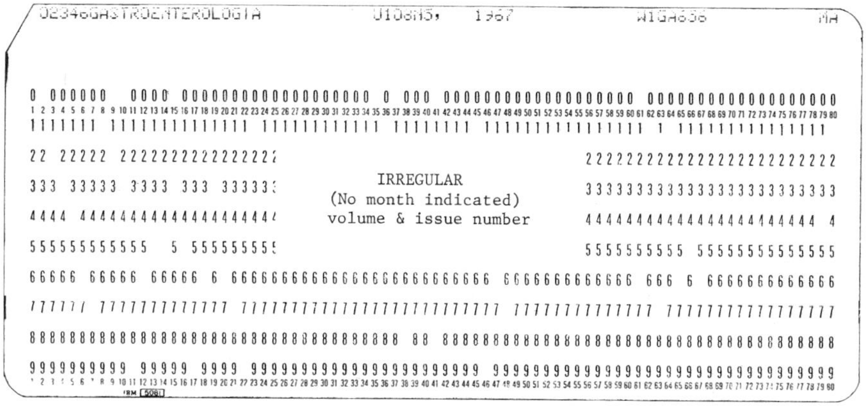

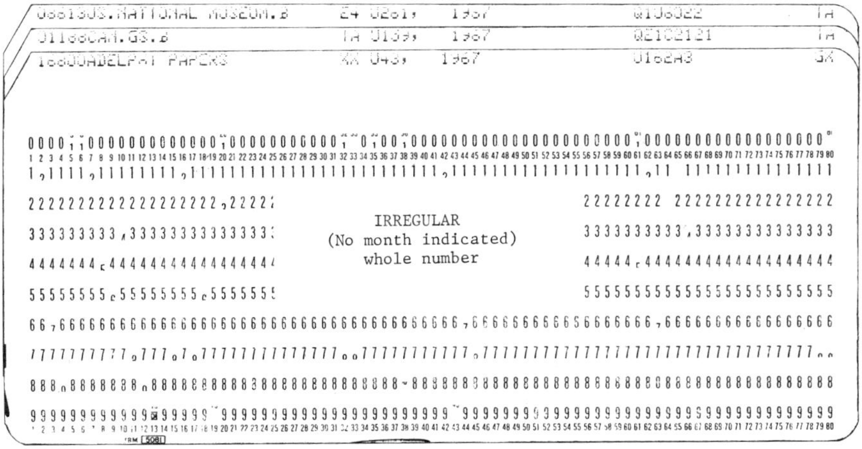

Figure 4 (Cont'd). Sample Expected Arrival Cards

these lists although a full title list could be made by going to the computer daily. This would also have eliminated some manual alphabetizing.

This system still required a certain amount of scratch keypunching. Irregularly received issues needed to have dates keypunched onto the update card. Multiple number issues required additional cards so that each number will be represented by a single update card. Serials which change their publication patterns in mid-volume require corrections to the master record and to the current or next update card. Corrections and additions also required proofreading.

Output. Three major print-outs or listings were products of the serials computer program and were regularly produced at prescribed intervals. They are shown in Figure 5 and I'll describe them briefly.

a. Master Tape Listing, Figure 5a. This is a listing of all the serial records arranged in alphabetical order by title, reproducing all of the information on the tape for each serial. These listings are indispensable to the serials clerks and are for internal use only. They are also used as proofsheets to locate errors.

b. Union or University Holdings List, Figure 5b. This list includes all serials in the University Library. It is alphabetically arranged by title and contains also call number, holdings record, information notes, see references, added entries and library location. Each branch library receives a copy each month, as well as the Serials Public Service Counter where the lists are displayed for public use. Additional copies can be prepared whenever desired. At the beginning of the new month the obsolete copies may be saved for use in serials acquisitions work or to be given to a neighboring library. The availability of a complete list of serials holdings, kept up-to-date monthly, is one of the chief advantages of the serials computer program. It eliminates many hours of clerical look-up when patrons want information on holdings.

c. Branch lists, Figure 5c. The format of these lists is standard for all branches. A branch list includes only holdings of serials for the given branch library or for the Central University Library. In format they resemble the union list except that location of current issues within the individual library is displayed instead of library location. These lists reflect each branch library's subject specialities and tend to be of significant value to the users because the lists exclude titles extraneous to their interests. Further specialized breakdowns by subjects, using classification, are, of course, possible.

d. Daily Arrivals Lists. A list of arrivals was generated daily and cumulated weekly to supplement the Branch Lists.

e. Bindery List. Upon demand, or as part of the monthly update procedures, cards for all complete, unbound volumes could be produced and listed. These cards had the update-card format except that the card listed only the bound volume, without parts. The cards were used to update the master tape when the bound volumes were returned from the bindery. The lists were utilized, first of all, to find

UNIVERSITY LIBRARY
UNIVERSITY OF CALIFORNIA, SAN DIEGO
SERIAL RECORD
MAY 1968

A-1

THE SERIAL RECORD IS AN ALPHABETICAL LISTING OF SERIAL TITLES IN THE UNIVERSITY LIBRARY. CALL NUMBERS APPEAR TO THE LEFT AND LOCATIONS TO THE RIGHT IN EACH COLUMN. HOLDINGS SHOWN ARE LOCATED IN ONE OF THE FOLLOWING LIBRARIES:

   CENTRAL UNIVERSITY LIBRARY (-CUL-)
   BIOMEDICAL LIBRARY (-BIOMED-)
   CLUSTER I LIBRARY (-CLUSTER I-)
   SCIENCE AND ENGINEERING LIBRARY (-S&E-)
   SCRIPPS INSTITUTION OF OCEANOGRAPHY LIBRARY (-SIO-)

LOCATIONS DESIGNATED CURRENT SHELVES AND DISPLAY SHELVES REPRESENT SHELVING OF THE LATEST ISSUES, WHEREAS, EARLIER HOLDINGS ARE LOCATED IN THE STACKS. AN ASTERISK (*) INDICATES THAT THE LATEST ISSUE IS ROUTED BEFORE SHELVING.

THE FOLLOWING ABBREVIATIONS DESCRIBE DIVISIONS WITHIN THE HOLDINGS STATEMENTS:

   S = SERIES NUMBER N = ISSUE NUMBER
   B = BOUND VOLUME P = PART NUMBER
   U = UNBOUND VOLUME SUPPL = SUPPLEMENT

Figure 5. Sample Printouts

```
1542            SH1A3404            +13305  0000  VIA E2                                                   X
ALASKA,DEPARTMENT OF FISH AND GAME,INFORMATIONAL LEAFLET$SH1A340$ALASKA,DEPT.FSH.INF. LFT$U1-24,U26-42,U44-156.
,(1951-    1971)*

                SH1A3407            +01963  0000  VIA E2
ALASKA,DEPARTMENT OF FISH AND GAME,RESEARCH REPORT$SH1A3407$ALK-FISH GAME,RES  REP$U1-7,(1956-        1969).

                QH1A341              +01964  0000  VI  E0
ALASKA,UNIVERSITY,BIOLOGICAL PAPERS$QH1A341$ALK.U.BIO PAPS$U2-12,(1958-         1969).

                SH1A3410                +12653                IA  D1
ALASKA FISHERIES,SH1A3410$ALASKA FISHERIE$$LIBRARY RETAINS ONLY LATEST TWO YEARS,SUBSERIES OF CURRENT FISHERIE
S STATISTICS,WHICH CUMULATES ANNUALLY INTO FISHERY STATISTICS OF THE UNITED STATES.

        M1AL128/GE/ST              +02066   0404  1MAY50        AAAA
ALASKA MEDICINE$M1AL128/GE/ST$ALASKA MEDICINE$U5N1-2,U86-8,U9,B10-11,U12-13,U14N1-2,(1963-APR1972).

        M1AL128/GE/ST              +21040  0404  1SA$50         RRRR
ALASKA MEDICINE$M1AL128/GE/ST$ALASKA MEDICINE$B1-5,U6N1,U9-13,U14N1-7,(1959-APR1972).

        F901A4                      +01967  0202  2GAD50        AAAA
ALASKA REVIEW$F901AA$ALASKA REVIEW$B1-2,U3-4,(1963-    1970).

        Q100U5A323                   +0196A  0001  VIA100        Z9XX
ALASKAN SCIENCE CONFERENCE,SCIENCE IN ALASKA,PROCEEDINGS$Q1B0U$A323$ALK SCI CONF,SCI-PROC$U1-10,B11-15,U16-17,
U19-22,(1950-   1971),LIBRARY HAS SUMMARIZED COMPLETE PROCEEDINGS OF FIRST CONFERENCE,1950,SHELVED WITH THIS S
ET.

        SH1A3427                    +17020                IA  4
ALBANIA,STAC!ONIT TE KERKIMEVE SHKENCORE TE EKONOMISE SE PESHKIMIT,BULETIN$SH1A3427$ALBANIA,STAC-EKON PESH,BSU
1,(1959-    1959).

        K1A394                                     +11656  0404  2GAD50        AAAA
ALBANY LAW REVIEW$K1A394$ALBANY LAW REVIEW$B30-39,U35,U36N1-3,(1946-       1972).

        M1AL170/GE                                 +02067  0303  2MAY50        AAAAJ11
ALBERT EINSTEIN MEDICAL CENTER,PHILADELPHIA,JOURNAL$M1AL170/GE$ALBERT EINSTEIN MED CR.J$B1-5,U6N4,B7-18,U19,U2
0N1,(1952-    1972)*

        M1AL170/GE                                 +21041  0303  2SA  E0
ALBERT EINSTEIN MEDICAL CENTER,PHILADELPHIA,JOURNAL$M1AL170/GE$ALBERT EINSTEIN MED CR.J$U1N4,B2-5,U6N2-4,B7-14
,U15-19,U20N1,(1953-   1972).

        GN1A4                       +33543                        GA  0
ALBERTA ANTHROPOLOGIST$GN1A1$$B1-2,(1967-DEC1968),CEASED WITH VOL.2,NO.3,DEC1968,SUPERSEDED BY WESTERN CANADIA
N JOURNAL OF ANTHROPOLOGY*

        F107546                     +09204   0404  1GAD50        AAAA
ALBERTA HISTORICAL REVIEW$F1075A6$ALBERTA HISTORICAL R$B13-17,U1A-19,U20N1-2,(1965-APR1972).

        QE1A342                     +08788                IA  0
ALBERTA SOCIETY OF PETROLEUM GEOLOGISTS,JOURNAL$QE1A342$ALBERTA  SC PET GEOL$U3-5,U6N2-11,B7-10,(1955-     1962),
CONTINUED BY BULLETIN OF CANADIAN PETROLEUM GEOLOGY,1963-*

        DA20A4                      +32085  0202  2GAD00        Z9XX
ALBION,PULLMAN,WASHINGTON,1869-    $DA2CA4$$B1-2,U3N4,(1945-   1971).
```

Figure 5a. Master List

FIGURE 5B CONTAINS THE SAME
INFORMATION DISPLAYED IN
FIGURE 5D ONLY IT IS
IN A ONE-COLUMN
FORMAT

Figure 5b. University List

Call Number	Entry	Location
AP 2 M66	MODERN QUARTERLY,NEW YORK B1-11,(1923-DEC1940) TITLE VARIES.VOLS.7-10 AS MODERN MONTHLY.SUBTITLE VARIES.SUSPENDED 1930-31 VOL.6,NO.4 NEVER PUBLISHED. CEASED WITH VOL.11 1940	-CUL- STACKS
PN 3321 M72	MODERN READING B15,(1947- 1947) CEASED WITH NO.23,1953	-CUL- STACKS
AP 8 M6	MODERN REVIEW,CALCUTTA,1907- B115-116,U117-118,B119-122,U123, U124N1-11,U125,U127,U128N1-2, (1964-FEB1971)	+ -CUL- STACKS
AP 2 M664	MODERN REVIEW,NEW YORK,1947-50 B1-3,(1947-JAN1950) CEASED WITH VOL.3,NO.2,JAN1950	-CUL- STACKS
AP 2 M665	MODERN REVIEW,MINCHESTER,MASSACHUSETTS, 1922-24 B1-2,(1922-JUL1924) CEASED WITH VOL.2,NO.3,JUL1924. UNITED WITH S4N REVIEW TO FORM MODERN S4N REVIEW	-CUL- STACKS
PG 3283 M6	MODERN RUSSIAN SHORT STORIES B1-2,(1968- 1969)	+ -CUL- STACKS
B 1 M6	MODERN SCHOOLMAN B1-47,U48N1-2,(1925- 1971)	+ -CUL- STACKS
AP 4 M615	MODERN SCOT U6N4,(1936-JAN1936) CEASED WITH VOL.6,NO.4,JAN1936. UNITED WITH SCOTTISH STANDARD TO FORM OUTLOOK,GLASGOW,1936-37	-CUL- STACKS
HX 1 M6	MODERN SOCIALISM B1,(1941- 1942) CEASED WITH VOL.1,NO.4,1942	-CUL- STACKS
	MODERN USES OF LOGIC IN LAW.SEE JURIMETRICS JOURNAL	-CUL-
AP 2 M6653	MODERN UTOPIAN,BERKELEY,CALIFORNIA,1966- U1-4,U5N4,(1966-JUL1971)	+ -CUL- SPECIAL COLLECTIONS
	MODERN UTOPIAN,MEDFORD,MASSACHUSETTS, 1966- .SEE MODERN UTOPIAN,BERKELEY, CALIFORNIA,1966-	-CUL-
HF 5381 M565	MODERN VOCATIONAL TRENDS REFERENCE HANDBOOK B6,(1963- 1963)	-CUL- LATEST IN REFERENCE
HC 10 M63	MODERN WORLD,COLOGNE U3,(1963- 1964) TRANSLATION OF SELECTED ARTICLES FROM MODERNE WELT	-CUL- STACKS
	MODERNA LIBRERIA RELIGIOSA.SEE DOCUMENTOS HISTORICOS DE MEJICO	-CUL-
PB 5 M6	MODERNA SPRAAK B58-60,U61,B62-63,U64,U65N1,(1964- 1971)	+ -CUL- STACKS
PB 5 M6L	MODERNA SPRAAK.LANGUAGE MONOGRAPHS U6-7,(1965- 1965)	-CUL- STACKS (ANALYZED)
	MOHAMMED 5 UNIVERSITE,RABAT.SEE RABAT, MOROCCO.JAMI AT MUHAMMAD 5	-CUL-
GN 2 M6	MOIS D ETHNOGRAPHIE FRANCAISE U2,U3N1-7,(1948- 1949)	-CUL- STACKS
AP 2 M6656	MOJO NAVIGATOR ROCK AND ROLL NEWS U1N12,U2N2,(1966-AUG1967)	-CUL- SPECIAL COLLECTIONS

Figure 5c. Branch List

Call Number	Entry	Location
W1 AL128	ALASKA MEDICINE U2N1-2,N6-8,U9,H10-11,U12-13, U14N1-2,(1963-APR1972)	+-BIOMED- STACKS
W1 AL128	ALASKA MEDICINE B1-5,U6N1,U9-13,U14N1-2, (1959-APR1972)	+-SOC U HOSP- STACKS
F 901 A4	ALASKA REVIEW B1-2,U3-4,(1963- 1970)	+-CUL- STACKS
Q 180 U5 A323	ALASKAN SCIENCE CONFERENCE.SCIENCE IN ALASKA.PROCEEDINGS U1-10,R11-15,U16-17,U19-22,(1950- 1971) LIBRARY HAS SUMMARIZED COMPLETE PROCEEDINGS OF FIRST CONFERENCE, 1950.SHELVED WITH THIS SET	+-SIO- STACKS
SH 1 A3427	ALBANIA.STACIONIT TE KERKIMEVE SHKENCORE TE EKONOMISE SE PESHKIMIT.BULETIN U1,(1959- 1959)	-SIO- STACKS
K 1 A394	ALBANY LAW REVIEW B30-34,U35,U36N1-3,(1966- 1972)	+-CUL- STACKS
W1 AL170	ALBERT EINSTEIN MEDICAL CENTER, PHILADELPHIA.JOURNAL B1-5,U6N4,B7-18,U19,U20N1,(1952- 1972)	+-BIOMED- STACKS
W1 AL170	ALBERT EINSTEIN MEDICAL CENTER, PHILADELPHIA.JOURNAL U1N4,B2-5,U6N2-4,B7-14,U15-19,U20N1, (1953- 1972)	+-SOC U HOSP- STACKS
GN 1 A4	ALBERTA ANTHROPOLOGIST B1-2,(1967-DEC1968) CEASED WITH VOL.2,NO.3,DEC1968. SUPERSEDED BY WESTERN CANADIAN JOURNAL OF ANTHROPOLOGY	-CUL- STACKS
F 1075 A6	ALBERTA HISTORICAL REVIEW B13-17,U18-19,U20N1-2,(19.5-APR1972)	+-CUL- STACKS
QE 1 A342	ALBERTA SOCIETY OF PETROLEUM GEOLOGISTS. JOURNAL U3-5,U6N2-11,B7-10,(1955- 1962) CONTINUED BY BULLETIN OF CANADIAN PETROLEUM GEOLOGY,1963-	-SIO- STACKS
DA 20 A4	ALBION.PULLMAN,WASHINGTON,1969- B1-2,U3N4,(1969- 1971)	+-CUL- STACKS
W1 AL180	ALBRECHT VON GRAEFES ARCHIV FUER KLINISCHE UND EXPERIMENTELLE OPHTHALMOLOGIE B168-180,U181-183,U184N1-2,(1965- 1972) CONTINUES ALBRECHT VON GRAEFS ARCHIV FUER OPHTHALMOLOGIE	+-BIOMED- STACKS
W1 AL188	ALBRECHT VON GRAEFFS ARCHIV FUER OPHTHALMOLOGIE.VEREINIGT MIT ARCHIV FUER AUGENHEILKUNDE B1-167,U168N1,(1854- 1965) TITLE VARIES,VOLS.1-16,1854-70, ARCHIV FUER OPHTHALMOLOGIE.MERGED WITH ARCHIV FUER AUGENHEILKUNDE, 1937,SUSPENDED NOV1944-AUG1947. CONTINUED BY ALBRECHT VON GRAEFES ARCHIV FUER KLINISCHE UND EXPERIMENTELLE OPHTHALMOLOGIE	-BIOMED- STACKS
AP 60 A23	ALCAZAR.TOLEDO,1936 B1-63,(1936- 1936) SUPPLEMENTS ACCOMPANY SOME ISSUES. CEASED WITH NO.63,27SEP1936	-CUL- SPECIAL COLLECTIONS
AP 2 A273	ALCHEMIST.MANHATTAN,KANSAS,1968- U1N1,(1968-OCT1968)	-CUL- SPECIAL COLLECTIONS
BX 5141 A1 A6	ALCUIN CLUB.COLLECTIONS B33-34,B38,(1938- 1952)	-CUL- STACKS (ANALYZED)
N 1 A18	ALDINE B9,(1878- 1879) TITLE VARIES,1868-1870 AS ALDINE PRESS.SUBTITLE VARIES	-CUL- STACKS

Figure 5d. New System University List

```
                                           SERIALS CUMULATED ARRIVALS LIST      OCT.08,1971 (10,2)                              PAGE   76

        G                                                                       AP2                                           ---4454A---
07087   LIFE                                                                    L547                                          ---6789AA--- AA
GO
                                           -909896    U71N11,10SEP1971          101971
                                           -909897    U71N12,17SEP1971          101971
                                           -909898    U71N13,24SEP1971          101971
                                           -909899    U71N14,01OCT1971          101971

09968   LINGUA NOSTRA                                                           PC1001                                         --1--1--1-1
GA                                                                              L5                                             --7--A----- AG
                                           -909962    U32N2,JUN1971             081971

29163   LISTENER,LONDON                                                         AP4                                            ---5445A---
GA                                                                              L5                                             -96678AA--- AA
                                           -909991    U86N2209,29JUL1971        101971
                                           -909992    U86N2210,05AUG1971        101971
                                           -909994    U86N2212,19AUG1971        101971
                                           -909995    U86N2213,26AUG1971        101971

06701   LISTY FILOLOGICKE                                                       P9                                             -----------
GA                                                                              L5                                             ---6---A---
                                           -909997    U94N2,    1971            071971

10614   LITERARY SKETCHES                                                       PS1                                            11111111111
GA                                                                              L5                                             --6789-A--- AA
                                           - 10614    U11N9,SEP1971             101971

13388   LITERATUR UND KRITIK                                                    PT1                                            -----------
GA                                                                              A9L5                                           ----7-8A--- AD
                                           -910004    U56,     1971             091971

06706   LITERATURE EAST AND WEST                                                PJ301                                          -----------
GA                                                                              L5                                             ----------- AA
                                           -910009    U14N4,    1970            061971
```

Figure 5e. New System Cumulated Arrivals List

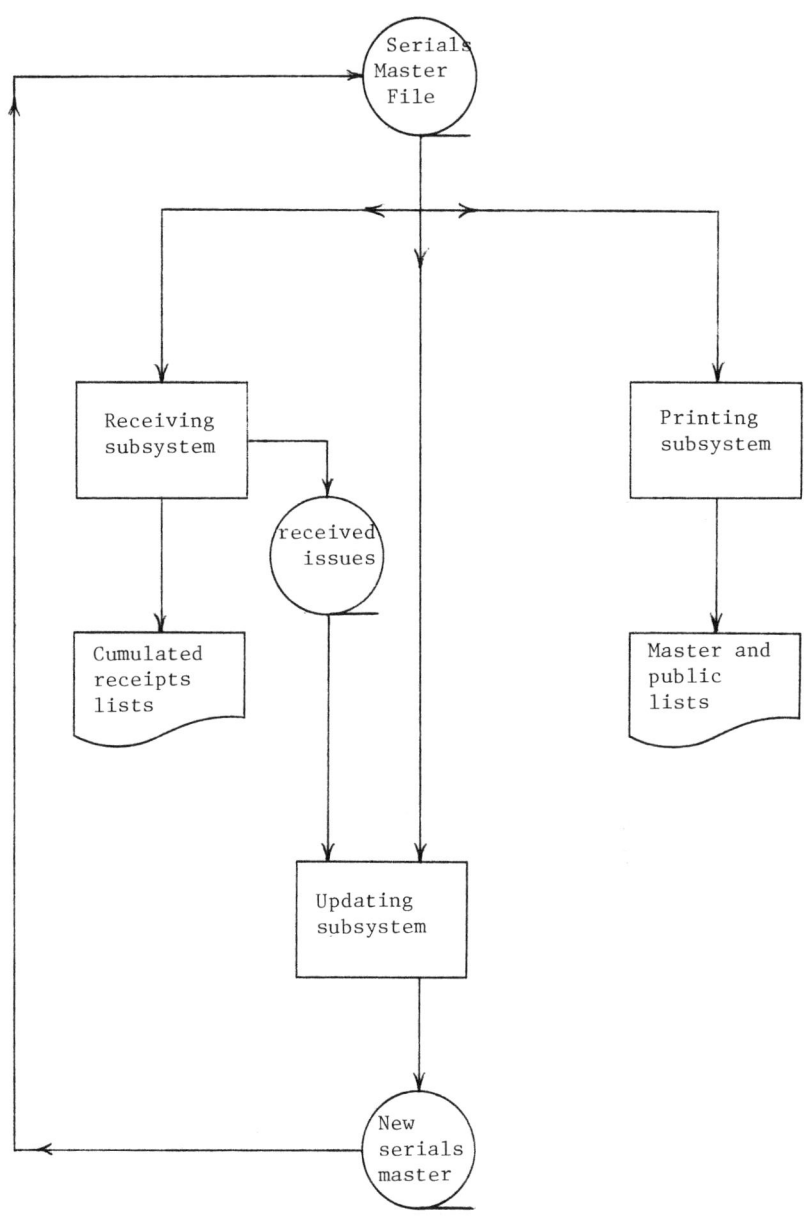

Figure 6. New System Flowchart

and collect complete, bindable volumes and then to transmit this information to central bindery preparation and the circulation desk.

f. Auxiliary listings.

(1) Pre-pass Error Listing. At the time of the monthly procedure the first listing available was a report of the pre-pass run. Incorrect additions were displayed, as were duplicate mnemonics. Corrections to the master tape could be made at this time or accumulated and entered in next update.

(2) Punch-list. After new titles and see references were added and after the corrections were made, the master tape was updated, producing the tape from which the pre-punched card deck of expected arrivals for the coming month was derived. This "punch" tape was listed and used to verify that the updating was correctly done. With this final check out of the way, the new arrival file was punched, interpreted, and ready for use.

(3) Update Corrections List. At the end of the update run a summation was printed showing the number of update cards and new titles processed, any errors in update cards, machine time for the update and the total number of entries or titles on tape.

(4) Statistics Listing. The statistics for the monthly branch lists appeared at the end of each list. They were summarized at the end of the union listing. These statistics included the number of see references and added entries, the number of inactive serial titles, the number of active (currently received) titles, the total number of serial titles and the total number of unit records on tape.

C. **Problems.**

A chronology of growth and other characteristics of the system is shown in Figure 1. The rapid growth factor was one of the major tests put to the system, since it was known in the beginning that the growth rate would be high. An average of from 300 to 400 titles had been added monthly for long periods of time.

One of the main problems that confronted the original system from 1964 to 1969 had to do primarily with the increased file size and activity. This situation was further aggravated by the lack of adequate program documentation and maintenance. Had there been a library systems staff available at the time to perform routine program maintenance and improvement, some of the problems encountered could have been alleviated. For example, the main up-date program was limited to handling 4000 arrivals. When over 4000 arrivals began coming in each month, the update operation was split in two by handling one-half of the alphabet in each pass. The suppression of the bindery routines was also caused by this same limitation since bindery cards are input along with the update cards.

Incomplete documentation contributed to this state of affairs because the flow diagrams lacked detail, and verbal descriptions were inadequate. Therefore, program changes were difficult to institute. Contributing also was the lack of continuing program maintenance.

This requires either very close cooperation with the campus computer center programming group or a minimum of a library programmer. Like a manual system which is seldom static, computer programs also require routine maintenance. And even if there is a systems group, the programming personnel are not always stable, especially if industry is on the other side of the campus waving high salaries around. Therefore, one must rely on good documentation to guarantee continuity throughout a program's lifetime.

The necessity for a two pass update and the suppression of bindery lists and cards were important problems confronted. The latter essentially nullified the bindery information update capabilities of the system, causing the bindery operation to revert back to the manual technique of going through the shelves to find completed volumes and converting the corresponding serials holdings records (unbound volume condition to bound) by the correction routines.

Some other lesser problems also surfaced. Sometimes the catalogers had to play games with the punctuation of entries in order to get them to file right. For example, agencies and titles can have similar entries which may interfile if care is not taken in the use of punctuation to keep titles together and agencies together.

Due to the fixed field length requirements of the punched update cards, call numbers were limited to 16 characters.

There was also some difficulty in coding the frequency since publishers do not always give it and since it changes without warning. This is an external problem which is, of course, prevalent in any serials system that predicts arrivals and/or assists in claiming.

Some of these problems, one may note, are system dependent while others might easily be prevalent in any system.

A most serious problem involved the use of mnemonic titles for check-in. The expected arrivals cards have 24 or less character mnemonics instead of full titles. Two things caused difficulty here. Some abrupt turnover in check-in personnel after a long period of stability in the group showed that the use of mnemonics made the system quite personnel dependent. Coupled with this factor was rapid growth adding many new mnemonic titles each month, sometimes at a pace faster than old ones could be learned.

Interfiling of monthly update cards into the file remaining from the previous month had become a major task, becoming more time consuming with growth. The serial identification numbers were not sequential with respect to the alphabetical listing of titles, and since the cards had only the mnemonics to use for filing, new personnel had difficult times.

A problem which showed up daily was the changes and corrections that occur, requiring scratch punching. Location changes from reference to stacks, classification changes altering call numbers, and activation of a previously inactive title are examples of corrections which required scratch punching and, therefore, more time consuming

operations than the simple check-in procedure of pulling a card.

Some serials (about 30) regularly arrived earlier than their predictions, with the result being an update card had to be scratch punched.

In dealing with irregular journals, although the month of publication may be irrevelant or not even specified, it had to be added to the volume and number in order to get a prediction card for the next issue. Of similar nature, serials called by season (i.e., fall, winter, spring and summer) were given a month instead of season in order that the programs be able to predict the next issues. One should remember that with irregulars the program really did not predict but merely replaced each update card with a new one for the next logical issue number in sequence.

It is apparent that some very irregular serial type publications cannot easily be accomodated automatically at all. One example is those which come numbered V1. − A, B, C, D, E and V2. − A, G, K etc., in which case it is impossible to know when to close a volume since some of the apparent issues will never be issued. Thus, a holdings statement can become very long.

Most of the following problems were recognized short-comings of the programs. Some of them are things which simply were not thought of during the design stage or else the programming required to handle them was felt to be too involved for the benefit derived.

If after arrival and check-in of a recent issue of a serial, it was reported missing, simple deletion from the latter record could cause it to be claimed. This would be a bigger problem if claiming was completely automated.

The program could only handle bound volumes which were complete and could not handle bound partial volumes. That is, if Volume 6, Nos. 1-6 were bound and Nos. 7 to 12 were not yet bound, the program would still show Nos. 1-6 as unbound. This causes some problems in knowing where to look since bound journals were automatically taken from current or display shelves and put into the stacks.

It was difficult for the check-in personnel to catch indexes, tables of contents, and title pages, which had effect on the binding logic since these are needed for binding. There is no panacea for this problem other than publisher conformity or consistency in issuance of these items.

Some serials come in individual issues but the last issue automatically comes as a bound volume, requiring disposal of the loose issues. In those cases the computer produces a bindery notice anyway which sometimes caused confusion. Now, there is a code that controls volumes which come bound and another code that indicates journals which are never to be bound.

Journals issued only by year with actual volume numbers were entered with volume numbers equal to the corresponding year of publication. On occasion, and this is not a rare occurrence, the journal

will start at some point, numbering the volumes, usually starting with Volume 1. This, needless to say, confuses the computer which tries to merge the most recent holdings before the older ones.

The programs did not handle serials with more than 99 issues per year in a straight forward fashion since only 2 characters were allowed in a fixed field to give the number of issues per year.

The programs did not predict the next logical issue number expected to arrive for a journal with say a 24-24 frequency code, i.e., 2 issues per month, when in working in pairs for each month one issue arrives early and is checked-in on a scratch punched card. For example, No. 13 and 14 were predicted and arrived. Now No. 15 also arrives. The next month's predicted arrivals will be No. 17 and 18, thus skipping 16. Of course, this is just another example of what routine system maintenance could have corrected upon discovery.

It is easy to look back and note deficiencies and lack of sophistication but the programs worked remarkably well when considering it was the earliest effort and tackled what many now believe is the most difficult library operation to automate. Perhaps the most remarkable fact of all is the reliability experienced over the years. The monthly update schedule was never aborted in over five years of regular operation.

III. TRANSITION

The timing of the arrival of a new computer on campus coincided with the increased pressures being exerted on the capacities of the original programs. Thus in late 1967, planning began to implement a new system on the computer, an RCA Spectra 70/Model 45. An added incentive to use the new computer was provided by its designation as an administrative machine to be used only for non-scientific purposes. This meant that the library should have ready access to it. (Note the *should*). In addition to problems of capacity, the original system programs for the CDC-3600 were difficult to alter due to many assembly language routines and sketchy documentation so that they would have to be rewritten, not converted.

In the new system we wanted to eliminate all of the problems noted and alleviate two kinds of personnel problems of concern to the serials librarian — 1) The problem that one faces when Helen and John have checked in serials for 28 years and both retire the same day; 2) The part-time student work force of 9 bodies putting in 11 hours each and turning over at the rate of 2 each month.

Both types of situations cause concern over the degree of personnel dependency which is endeared to a system. Having lived for the first few years with high staff stability, and then confronting some rapid turnover, we decided to design a system and procedures which would allow for rapid training of personnel and relatively quick attainment of competency. We also kept an eye out for variety in the average

workday so that the employees would have some flexibility in laying out their own work routines.

These were some of the human factors. We were also pretty concerned about the programs, their documentation (or lack thereof), flexibility to accomodate requested changes, and their efficiency in terms of computer costs.

The programs, their capabilities, and the methods and formats of input and output, would of course, dictate to a great extent the types of manual procedures that would be associated with the new system.

So let's look at the new system, which is the one in current operation.

IV. THE NEW SYSTEM
A. Design Considerations:

In addition to expanding the sheer magnitude of its handling capacities, provision for other improvements was just as important and necessary.

The original system utilized IBM cards for the check-in operation. In order to fit all the needed check-in data for a single issue onto one 80 column punched card, the title was abbreviated in mnemonic form. With 24 columns thus devoted to the mnemonic title, the rest of the check-in card contained the serial identification number, call number, library, location (stacks, display shelves, etc.) issue designation (volume number, date) and the dealer or vendor code. We wanted to get away from the constraints of the old 80 column card syndrome.

The demands placed on the check-in personnel regarding mnemonics were beginning to surface as a problem because of the close to 20,000 titles in the file. Therefore, to make the system less personnel dependent and to allow for continued growth, mnemonics had to be eliminated. There is no magic number as to the number of titles that can be checked in using 24 character mnemonics, but with reasonably good mnemonics, 10,000 titles were still being handled. Probably, efficiency begins a sharp decline after 4000 or 5000 active titles.

Abolition of mnemonics meant a method had to be devised to handle full titles which range up to several hundred characters in length. Two were investigated. One obvious possibility was to create a list of expected arrivals each month instead of a file of cards. The other was to print on top of the cards (using prepunched, continuous roll stock, or IBM's multi-function card machine); this allows about 2000 characters of print with 80 machine readable characters. The list method does not result in a machine readable record, thus requiring a second step; e.g., the pulling of cards containing punched transaction numbers identical to the transaction numbers on the list. In this case an expected arrival listed on the transaction list would be "checked-in" when a card with the matching transaction number was processed by the computer against the transaction file. The cumulation of daily receipts registered on the transaction file (magnetic tape) would serve to update the master file.

We looked at one possibility of eliminating the second step of pulling the transaction cards parallel to marking the transaction list (also known as the predicted arrivals list). It involved the use of a score sheet type of arrangement in which mark sensing equipment would be used. Without further explanation, however, the idea was dropped when equipment test data available on mark sensing devices at that time indicated that a minimum error rate of several percent could be expected. Obviously, serial records could not tolerate that degree of uncertainty.

The use of on-line terminals to check-in serials represented a serious possibility due to several inherent advantages, including most prominently the capability for immediate change of records and ability to facilitate file maintenance activities with relative ease. However, a cost analysis showed that an on-line check-in system would be too expensive. Why? First, with only 400 to 500 transactions per day occurring with 12,000 active titles at the time, expensive terminals would be setting idle too much of the time. Also, with a terminal required for each check-in person, the average terminal "on time" would be reduced yet further. Finally, with plans for decentralized check-in, terminals would be needed at each branch library. The latter factor killed the concept until the day money would be no object, or costs of on-line operation were significantly reduced.

Finally, the list method of check-in was selected. It offered inherent advantages of providing an immediate positive record of arrivals by virtue of the fact that each arrival is marked off the list as it is checked-in. Perhaps a more important reason, however, is the fact that a list can be scanned, whereas a card file cannot be visually scanned at all. Time studies proved the value of this approach when the "finding time" of a title on a list was found to be nearly half that of a card file. The list is especially effective for foreign titles which are not always readily discernible. Another consideration involved the question of reliability concerning whether the printing being done on prepunched continuous roll stock could be kept in phase with the transaction numbers (i.e., if the card with the punched transaction number, 4065, is to correspond with "ABC Magazine V.6, No. 5, June 1969", then the 4065th record must be printed on top of the 4065th transaction card). When printing a file the size of 20,000 records it is possible to skip a record thus throwing the printed card record out of synchronization. Also the printing time is higher per record when one compares the time to print the same amount of data on a 132 character line (list) with an 80 character line (cards).

A decision had been made to decentralize the check-in operation for selected branch libraries. The list adapted well to this requirement also. Although the Central Serials Department had always guaranteed and delivered serials to the branch libraries within 24 hours of their arrival, expansion of the campus and increasing distances made accomodation of decentralized check-in a desirable feature in the new system.

Decentralizing serials receiving entails a number of problems which were soluble with a list but further complicated by any attempts to use the card check-in method. First, the problem of getting addresses changed is not accomplished overnight, and the time lag often stretches into years before all addresses are corrected by publishers and vendors. Therefore, for the system to operate smoothly, every expected arrival must be capable of being checked-in at either of two locations — its branch library location or at Central Serials. This is not as serious if only one copy of a given title is expected, but when multiple copies of a title are received for two or more libraries, then it becomes clear that some central control must be retained.

An on-line real-time system would solve this problem nicely since receipts would be registered and the information made available immediately through terminals. This would prevent both Central Serials and a branch library from attempting to check-in copies of the same issue of a serial and crediting it to the same library.

With the list method this problem is circumvented a little differently. The list for Central Serials would contain all predicted arrivals. The branch library would have a partial list containing only items that should be addressed to them. Thus, both the branch library and Central Serials are given the same transaction numbers for a given title and issues. To work smoothly, only one branch library at a time can be permitted to decentralize its serials receiving. Every issue of a multiple copy title checked-in at Central Serials is queued to the other branch libraries (those not yet doing their own check-in operation) before checking-in the last copy for the decentralized branch. Since each transaction marked off on the list requires a congruent transaction card to be pulled for later input, the transaction card file is placed in Central Serials and the branch receipts are either called in (for small branches), or their list brought to Central Serials daily to pull transaction cards. Thus the list serves as a buffer between initial check-in and creation of the machine readable input (i.e., pulling the transaction card). The absence of a given transaction card in the file would indicate that the issue in question has already been checked-in and any further reference to it means an unwanted duplicate copy has arrived.

Perhaps it is not apparent that decentralized card files would not work with appropriate procedural and program checks; however, the problem of multiple handling and other delays becomes evident as one looks into the many idiosyncracies of serial control.

There was much speculation at the beginning of the design study that we should use the serial identification number to sequence the titles and cross-references. It was decided to keep the accession type of serial identification number and continue letting the programs file titles. No serious problem had been experienced in the past with machine filing, and there was the added benefit to be considered of having a unique identification number for each title — a tag that never

changes. By keeping the identification numbers constant, any subsequent accounting system would be able to interface with the serials system using the identification numbers as the common element.

Moving on to another area of concern brings up the important aspect of predicting arrivals. The old program would generate a card for each issue of a serial expected during the month — when the serial in question was defined as "regular". A "regular" serial was one that had equal time intervals between issues (i.e., monthly, weekly, quarterly, etc.) As mentioned before, this was an unnecessarily restrictive definition since there are many serials that have predetermined publication patterns which do not involve equal time intervals. For this reason it was decided to add a 12 month prediction calendar as part of the fixed field data in the serials record. By doing this we could bring another 40% of our file into the realm of predictable regulars; this would boost to approximately 80% the proportion of titles that would have predictable publication patterns. With 80% of the file classed as regular, one can then begin to think about writing algorithms for automatic or computer assisted claiming. One of my major concerns in a computer assisted serials control system has to do with the simple fact that if you cannot accurately predict arrivals, you certainly cannot automate claiming — except for the simple skipped issue type of cases.

At this point in the design studies it became clear that we could solve another deficiency of the old system — a lack of receipt history. By paralleling a receipt calendar with the prediction calendar, we could compile receipt data (See Figure 7). Check-in personnel would now have a graphic representation of a journal's arrival behavior.

It should be pointed out that for those serials which were already regular, the old frequency and regularity codes could be used to generate the predicted arrival calendar. For the others it would be necessary to go back and manually key-in the calendar data for each appropriate title.

The twelve month calendars (as can be seen in Figure 7) or specifically the publication pattern and the receipt pattern, offer several important advantages.

The receipt pattern may change as each month's receipt data replaces the year-old data. In actual practice, after enough receipt information is accumulated and evaluated, it would be possible to compute an arrival delay code or shift code to adjust the appearance of predictions on the list. This could serve to refine the prediction process to a point where automatic claiming can be considered at least feasible. As more experience is obtained with the calendars, the receipt data being cumulated for irregulars (receipt data is collected automatically for all active titles) can be mapped into the blank prediction calendars, thus becoming the assumed publication pattern. It would also eliminate some of the manual efforts required in converting many of the old "irregular" serials into the new broader definition of "regular" and assist in the claiming efforts in the future by providing better control

SERIALS EXPECTED ARRIVALS LIST   FEB.1972 (2,2)   PAGE   771

20636   INTERNATIONAL JOURNAL OF HEALTH EDUCATION   M1
MA S   IN796
                              -908649   U14N4,   1971   021972   --1--1--1--1
                                                                                                             --7-------- AA
                                                                                                                0404   2

31720   INTERNATIONAL JOURNAL OF HEALTH SERVICES   M1
MA S   IN798
                               908650   I2N1,FEB1972   021972   -1--1--1--1
                                                                                                             ------C--1- AA
                                                                                                                0404   1

00347   INTERNATIONAL JOURNAL OF HEAT AND MASS TRANSFER   QC1
EB S   1636
                              -908651   U14N12,DEC1971   021972   11111111111
                                 15ML JAN72   --66789AAC1- AA
                                                                                                                1212   1

06242 -INTERNATIONAL JOURNAL OF HEAT AND MASS TRANSFER   QC1
I   S   1636
                              -908652- U14N12,DEC1971   021972   11111111111
                                 15ML JAN72   --66789AAC1- AA
                                                                                                                1212   1

02801   INTERNATIONAL JOURNAL OF LEPROSY   M1
MA S   IN803
                               908653   U39N2,JUN1971   111971   -1--1--1--1
                              - 02801   U30,DEC1962   EXP'12-72   021972   --A-------6 AA
                                                                                                                0404   1

29541   INTERNATIONAL JOURNAL OF LEPROSY   M1
SA S   IN803
                               908654   U39N2,JUN1971   111971   -1--1--1--1
                                                                                                             --A-------6 R8
                                                                                                                0404   1

31721   INTERNATIONAL JOURNAL OF MAN MACHINE STUDIES   TA167
GA S   15
                               908655   U3N4,OCT1971   121971   1--1--1--1-
                                                                                                             ----------- Z9
                                                                                                                0404   1

20490   INTERNATIONAL JOURNAL OF MASS SPECTROMETRY AND ION PHYSICS   QC1
EB S   16365
                               908656   U6N1,JAN1971   071971   11111111111
                                                                                                             ---A9BCCC26 R1
                                                                                                                0612   1

Figure 7. New System Expected Arrivals List

over the predictions. The latter affects the efficiency of the transaction list by providing a cleaner file with fewer transactions being carried for such things as annuals that are often carried as an expected arrival for the 11 months following each receipt of an issue.

The calendars may even hold more possibilities which have not yet been exploited.

Questions have been raised over our decision to use a monthly time frame. Some feel this is not accurate enough to allow automatic claiming later on. Past experience with the old serials system indicates otherwise, however. Control which is too fine cannot be justified since the fine tuning of weekly or daily correlations does not lend itself to the many esoteric and erratically behaved serial titles which are received in any academic research library. Also, sporadic mail tie-ups, longshoreman strikes, etc., all contribute to the futility of trying to predict arrivals too accurately.

The reasoning outlined above is also apparent in the capabilities built into the receipt pattern. When a serial is issued more frequently than monthly, it is obvious that the simple mode of tabulating the receipt data can only indicate whether none, or one or more issues predicted to arrive in a given month, did indeed arrive. For example, if 2 issues are expected and only one arrives, the receipt calendar would simply show that something predicted that month did arrive in the same month. There is no way to indicate the month or months of arrival for the stragglers. In any case, we do not want to shift our predictions because only part of the predictions are arriving late. It is far better to expect them prematurely, and thereby have them on the transaction list for simple check-in, rather than to shift into a later month and frequently have to punch scratch cards. Again, our experience indicated to us that the returns were already beginning to diminish if we attempted finer control.

The basic premise of our whole prediction system is the assumption that the publication pattern and the issue designation correlate with each other. The new system uses this as the point of reference as did the original system.

These somewhat detailed descriptions are only examples of the types of considerations which were repeated many times during the course of our review and redesign efforts.

B. Description

The new system has been in operation since 1969, but fill implementation of all features has been a gradual process, with some improvements still being made. Basically the system is operating as designed with few modifications.

Early in 1969, the RCA Spectra 70/45 computer, for which the new programs were written, was removed from campus with only 6 weeks notice. Therefore, until the computer situation became stable, we were limiting our development activities. At that point I might add that the serials system was still running, not because of, but in spite of

the computer! A stripped down version of the system was in operation using an off campus RCA Spectra 70. (The situation concerning lack of stability and scheduling of computers is a national phenomena in the U.S. It has contributed significantly to development and operating costs through conversion requirements, and has generally slowed progress. I often point out to computer center personnel that the library is tied to scheduling — the books come in the books go out, hourly, daily, and weekly, thereby requiring the same stability as any banking institution expects.)

Current operation of the UCSD serials processing system is performed on a Burroughs' B-6700 computer. The system performs most of the same functions accommodated by the original system, but with many of the design improvements covered earlier. Primary changes are reflected in the use of a check-in list or the expected arrivals list (See Figure 7), keying in of transaction numbers for input of receipt data, and the addition of receipt and prediction calendars. Also other procedures and features have been streamlined or otherwise improved upon.

The following discussion summarizes the operating characteristics of the current serials system. For a more complete and detailed description, the reader is referred to the recent LARC report written by Earl Balch, Systems Programmer/Analyst at the UCSD Library.[3]

1. General Discussion.

The new (or current) UCSD Library's serials processing system consists of three subsystems. Each includes computer operations and associated manual procedures that utilize computer products or produce computer input data and are directly related to the operation of the system. The receiving, updating, and printing subsystems (see Figure 6) operate independently during a basic monthly cycle following separate processing schedules. There is, however, information being passed between the subsystems such that an event occurring in one subsystem may cause an event in another. The primary functions of the subsystems are:

Receiving — record the arrival of serials being received by the library;

Updating — maintain a current record of serials held by the library including location and holdings;

Printing — produce printed lists of serials information for the users and staff of the library.

At any time during a system cycle, one or more of the subsystems can be active and processing serials information. Assuming the existence of the serials master file, which is common input to each subsystem, it is possible to step through a cycle to describe the various events that occur.

Although receiving serials is a continuous operation, there is a point at which a new updated master file is available. It then becomes necessary to refresh the data in the receiving subsystems. This data is

displayed on a printed list which is used to record receipts.

Serials are checked-in when received using an expected arrivals list containing an entry for each active serial record. Predicted issues appear on the list (see Figure 7) with transaction numbers which are marked upon receipt of the designated serial issue. These transaction numbers are later keyed (see Figure 8 for samples) and input to a computer program. Unexpected arrivals are recorded by volume, issue number, and date on the list. They are later keyed at the same time as the transaction numbers using the serial identification numbers for the titles along with the issue descriptions.

The records and information on this list must correspond with the master file. Therefore, when the data is refreshed, received transactions are purged, deleted records are removed, new records are added, and new issues are predicted. These changes to the list are effected by processing a disk file of which the list is a printed representation. At the same time the expected arrivals list is generated, the printing subsystem is required to output new printed lists.

The printing subsystem decodes and arranges the information in the serials master file before printing the various lists that will be used by library patrons and staff. The final products are bound and then distributed to reference desks, branch libraries, decentralized processing stations, and staff members.

Serials information for the master file is continually changing throughout the cycle. New records are being created while existing records are being changed and received issues are being accumulated in the receiving subsystem. As in the original system, manual preparation of an intermediate serial record (ISR) initiates the task of adding a new record. Changes or corrections to records already in the file similarly begin with the preparation of a correction form (same format as ISR but on paper instead of card stock). ISR and correction forms are visually checked for format and content and then keypunched. The punched cards are processed by computer programs to list and check the data. After correcting the data, the cards are reprocessed to create input files which are used to update the master file.

At the proper time in the system cycle, received issue data is passed from the receiving subsystem to the updating subsystem. This data and the other input (new records, changes, and corrections) are used to update the master file. Once this is accomplished a new cycle begins.

The cycle period (one month in this case) is determined by the need for current information balanced by the cost of operating the system and the actual time required to complete the necessary tasks.

2. Computer Processes.

A Burroughs B-6700 computer system, operated by the UCSD Computer Center, is used for the serials computer operation. The B-6700 is a large multi-programmed multi-processing system capable of handling batch, remote batch and interactive jobs at the same time. Most of the processing is done in standard batch mode.

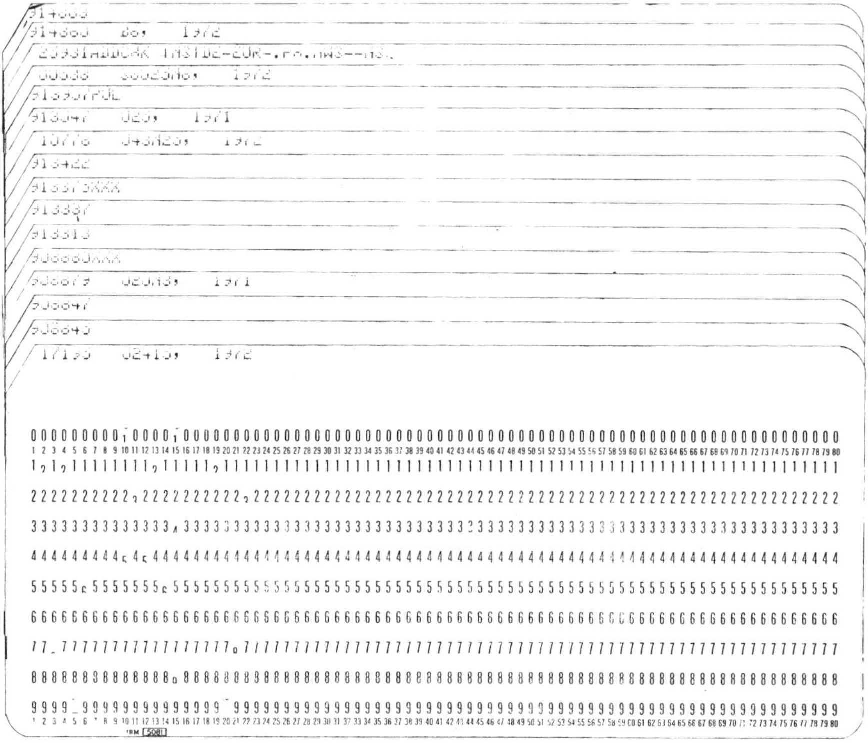

Figure 8. New System Expected Arrival Cards.

A batch mode job is presented to the system as a deck of punched cards containing control cards and may contain one or more files of data. The cards are read and the job is placed on high-speed disk (one head per track). Execution is initiated by the system as soon as possible. Operators make tapes available when requested by the job, but existing disk files must be present upon first access by a program. New disk files are created as specified by the programs with the system assigning the necessary disk space. Files are normally saved on disk and copied to tape.

All printer output for a job is written to disk or tape backup files. Backup disk files are printed slowly after the job terminates, while backup tapes are printed later upon request from the user.

Burroughs B-6700 COBOL, which conforms to CODASYL-68 standards (contains B-6700 extensions), was used to program the UCSD Serials Processing System. The object code files from compiled programs are stored on tape. When jobs are run, the programs to be executed are first copied from tape to disk and removed after execution.

Because of their size, the disk space rental charge and the relative infrequency of access, disk files used by the serials system are saved on tape after creation or update, thereby freeing large disk areas for other use.

Thirty tapes are used to store old, current, and backup serials information and as new information supersedes old, tapes are scratched and assigned to a pool of available tapes. When a new file is to be written, a corresponding tape is assigned to store the output. Tape files are written directly to tape, but disk files must be copied to tape after they are written.

There are three major files in the serials system. The serials master file contains fixed length, blocked records. It is a tape file because of its size (over 30,000 records) and the fact that the whole file must be read at different times during the system cycle. The transaction file, about half the size of the master, is a disk file which is accessed repeatedly during jobs that are run several times a month. The records in this file are variable in length and are composed of as many small fixed length segments as needed. The edit file is also a disk file containing variable length records. But here, the records are packed into a fixed length block until the next record will not fit.

Duplication and reconstruction capability are provided for the serials master and transaction files. This is important because of the significant investment in time and money that have been expended to maintain the information in these files. Duplicates of the current files are kept in the library in the event that something happens to the files at the computer center. Files and input from the previous cycle are also saved so that the current files can be reconstructed should this be necessary.

3. Check-in Procedures.

The following steps outline the process involved when a serial issue is received and checked-in.
   a. Find record on list using full entry.
   b. Compare issue designation to predictions.
   c. If a match is made then indicate receipt on the list by marking a red line (———) to the left of the transaction numbers that corresponds to the issue received.
   d. If some of the predicted data is wrong then line out and indicate the correct information to the right (make corrections to the master record as required).
   e. If no match is made then add the issue to the list as a received issue to be keypunched using the serial ID number and the issue designation; as many as 40 issues may appear for a given title; (note — if any prediction is totally wrong and such an issue does not exist, the prediction should be removed from the list by lining out the issue designation and writing "PUL" in red to the left of the transaction number; if any data is in error due to frequency change, etc., indicate correct information then write "COR" in red to the left of the transaction number).
   f. If the entry is not found on the list, follow alternate procedure.
   g. At the end of each check-in day, punch transaction cards; information to be punched is indicated in red; after punching, the cards are checked against the list and black lines are drawn over the red marks to show that the information has been punched; use appropriate action codes and date as required; keep cards in order as it may be necessary to locate a card later.
   h. Each week new check-in lists and cumulated receipt lists are printed as required following transaction file update.
   i. Each month follow update procedure for master tape.
   j. A special tape of all received issues is submitted to program "SERIALUPDMASTER" each month to add received issues to holdings.
   k. Any active title that is deleted from the master file must have a "DELETE" card made to remove that record from the transaction file during generation of the new transaction file after updating the master file.
   l. Beginning with the second month the check-in list will be able to provide the following information for use in claiming:
      1) next expected issues
      2) publication pattern and month of receipt
      3) month and year prediction was made
      4) source and claims action code
      5) after a claim has been made there will be an indication of the month claimed or followed-up.
   m. Each week the claims clerk should provide a list of those issues claimed; a "C" and a red line to the right of the issue designation on the check-in list indicates that a claim has been

made; after the claim has been keypunched a black line is drawn over the red line.
n. Weekly receipts lists or superseded check-in lists may be passed to the claims clerk to provide claim receipt data. Using the graph time frame (i.e., the calendars) at the right side of the list, the clerk can determine whether a given issue has been claimed ("X") and if a followup claim has been made ("F"). The position of these codes on the time frame indicates the month in which the action was taken. The presence of a receipt flag indicates that a claimed issue has been received.

Transaction cards are keypunched in the following format:

Columns
 1- 6 Transaction number (6 digits) or space followed by serial ID number (5 digits).
 7- 9 Action code.
 10-39 Issue designation and/or comment (appears on list).
 40-69 Optional-use for short title or comment (does not appear on list).
 70-75 Date of prediction.
 76 Use "F" if follow-up to claim is made.
 77-78 Month of claim if other than current month.
 79-80 Not used.

V. REVIEW

A. Staffing and Costs

Figure 1 gives representative figures for computer and paper costs during different periods of the system's operation. Previous studies on some of the labor costs involved in the computer assisted serials operation were reported by M. J. Voigt in a 1963 article.[4] The results indicated check-in costs were essentially identical for manual serials records as for the expected arrival card system used in the computer operation. Since then, going to list check-in cut 50% off of the original system's check-in time (per issue handled) plus savings in filing. The size of the check-in staff has essentially been reduced by one FTE over the years while increasing the workload from 5000 to 14,000 active subscriptions.

B. Commentary

The library users, faculty, students, and librarians, are quite happy with the system. In fact, it has been noted that when users want serial information they seldom refer to the card catalog even for call numbers. Most users have never had direct access to the serials holdings information before and they have in general become enthusiastic supporters of the printed book catalog type of serials holdings information. As an example, in the process of converting to a new computer we were forced into reprogramming the printout module first since the old IBM 1401 was to be removed from the CDC 3600

computer system. In the short notice given, we were only able to get out the university list without any individual branch lists. This brought immediate reaction from users indicating their definite dependence upon the serials printouts.

The branch libraries offer a spectra of opinions ranging from ecstatic enthusiasm for the system to mild criticism of some aspects. On the ecstatic side are the branches which like having their complete holdings kept up to date with no effort on their part, and they get the fringe benefits of having knowledge of all the other libraries' holdings, too. In the middle is the branch which would like to at least do its own claiming. Then comes the branch that feels the guaranteed less-than-24-hour delivery service of Central Serials is a bit optimistic. They would rather have the journals as soon as they arrive in the mail and are willing to check-in and claim within their own organization. Their comments often include the statement that they have many calls from faculty for recent journal issues that they feel would be better to have delivered directly.

Other branch complaints concern the fact that they do not know what has been claimed. Also they feel they are more familiar with their journals and could catch title changes and other elements which sometimes need correction.

Experience with the Biomedical Library performing its own decentralized check-in operation indicates that it is highly desirable to have catalogers nearby who can assist check-in personnel when such things as title changes do occur or are thought to have occurred.

Certainly, successful application of the computer in the area of serials processing and control would not have been possible at UCSD were it not for the pioneering efforts of all involved. To program the kinds of details involved in the system required a lot of homework in order to understand all of the possibilities that might be confronted during routine operations, and to establish viable boundary conditions to control just how much should be designed into the system. I.E., the system does not contain unnecessary complexities which could have caused more trouble than they were worth. That little fact, in itself, is something worth considering in any endeavor which contains as many idiosyncracies as the nature of serial publications.

REFERENCES

1. Vdovin, George, et. al., "Computer Processing of Serial Records," *Library Resources and Technical Services*, Vol. 7, No. 1, Winter 1963, pp. 71-80.

2. Vdovin, George D., Newman, C. Perry, and M. J. Voigt. *Final Report — Serials Computer Project.* University Library and Computer Center. UCSD La Jolla, California, May, 1964.

3. Balch, Earl, "Serials Processing System Reference Manual," *The LARC Reports*, Vol. 5/Issue 3, 1972.

4. Voigt, M. J., "The Costs of Data Processing in University Libraries — in Serials Handling," *College & Research Libraries*, Vol. 24, pp. 489-491, 1963.

Other Published Sources of Information on the UCSD Serials System

Bosseau, Don L., "The University of California at San Diego Serials System — Revisited," *Program*, Vol. 4, No. 1, Jan. 1970, pp. 1-29.

Bosseau, Don L., "The Computer in Serials Processing and Control," in *Advances in Librarianship*, Vol. 2, 1971. Seminar Press, N.Y.

APPENDIX

LARC AUTOMATED SERIALS SYSTEMS INSTITUTE
Chase-Park Plaza, St. Louis, Missouri
May 24-25, 1973

PARTICIPANTS

R. E. Utman
Systems Development Librarian
Princeton University

Ms. Marilyn Fletcher
Library
University of New Mexico

Mrs. Britt Kjolstad
Acquisitions Section
United Nations Library

Mrs. Jean S. Lee
Assistant Librarian
A. W. Calhoun Medical Library
Emory University

Mr. Mark G. Knoblauch
Head, Serials Department
Chicago Public Library

Mr. John A. Kopper
Serials Librarian
Mayo Clinic Library

Ms. Joan Evelyn Barry
Serials Librarian
University of Sydney Library
Sydney, NSW, Australia

Mr. Frank Orser
Assistant Chairman, Serials
University of Florida Libraries

Mr. William T. O'Malley
Acting Associate University
   Librarian
University of Rhode Island Library

Mr. Isidro Guzman, Jr.
Pan American University Library
Edinburg, Texas

Mr. Harry C. Broussard
Head, Serials Department
Northern Illinois University

Mrs. B. Jarkiewicz
Serials Librarian
Ontario Institute for Studies in
   Education Library
Toronto, Ontario, Canada

Mrs. R. Wolfe
Head of Technical Services
Ministry of Education, Ontario
Toronto, Ontario, Canada

Mr. Gary N. Denue
Assistant Director for Technical
   Processes
Chester Fritz Library
University of North Dakota

Ms. Helen Wilkinson
Assistant Cataloger
Eastern Michigan University Library

Ms. Twyla Mueller
Eastern Michigan University Library

Mr. James Heilik
National Science Library
Ottawa, Ontario, Canada

J. Terry Moore
Serials Librarian
New Orleans Public Library

Ms. Clairann Schickler
University of Washington Library

Ms. Odette Shepherd
Indiana University Library

Ms. Shere Connan
Indiana University Library

Miss Lesley Clarke
International Development Research
   Center
Ottawa, Ontario, Canada

Miss Idair Smookler
Librarian
Union Carbide Corporation
Charleston, West Virginia

Ms. Suzanne E. DeCarre
US Naval Oceanographic Office
Suitland, Maryland

Ms. Elizabeth R. Harrington
Director, Research Libraries
Arthur D. Little, Inc.
Cambridge, Massachusetts

Ms. Mildred F. Hallowitz
Serials Librarian
Health Sciences Library
State University of New York
 at Buffalo

Mr. Ed Buchinski
Head, Canadian MARC Office
National Library of Canada

Mrs. Dorothy B. Roeske
Director of Libraries
Principia College

Ms. Nancy Olson
System Analyst
Mankato State College

H. J. Schwartz
University of Guelph Library
Guelph, Ontario, Canada

Mr. Philip M. Calcagno
Serials Librarian
Southern Illinois University

Mr. Robert S. Rodriguez
University of Texas at San Antonio

Mr. John Thornbury
Serials Librarian
Norris Medical Library
Los Angeles, California

Ms. Paula Mortensen
Systems Analyst
Data Processing Center
University of New Mexico

Mr. James E. Raper
Head, Technical Services
The Medical Library Center of
 New York

Mr. Spencer S. Marsh
Director, Union Catalog of Medical
 Periodicals
The Medical Library Center of
 New York

Mrs. Suzanne Nagy
Library
University of Missouri

Mr. Charles J. Schmidt, Director
Middle Georgia Regional Library
Macon, Georgia

Mr. Ryburn M. Ross, Assistant Director
Technical & Automated Services
Cornell University Libraries

F. L. Slater, Manager
Library Systems Development
University of Pittsburgh

Mr. Jeffrey E. Pimper
Lawrence Livermore Laboratory L-366

Mrs. Rue E. Olson
1701 Towanda Avenue
Bloomington, Ill.

Ms. Nancy P. Sanders
Head, Serial Records
Arizona State University

Mrs. Marion C. Playfoot
7512 Bauman Avenue
Omaha, Nebraska

Mrs. Judy Wells
1901 Minnehaha No. 309
Minneapolis, Minnesota

Mr. Robert L. Lormand
Lawrence Livermore Laboratories

Ms. A. Elizabeth Crosby
Cornell University Libraries

Ms. Elaine T. Dunatov
5-143 Coordinated Science Laboratory
University of Illinois at Urbana-
   Champaign

Mr. Kevin McShane
Serials Librarian
American Museum of Natural History
New York, New York

Ms. Susan Hood
Med Tronic, Inc.
Minneapolis, Minn.

LARC Headquarters Staff

Post Office Box 27235
Tempe, Arizona 85282

Mr. Frank S. Patrinostro, Executive Secretary
Mr. Michael J. Wagner, Administrative Assistant

INSTITUTE FACULTY

WARREN BIRD, Duke University Medical Library

B.S. Georgetown University, 1956 (Physics)
M.L.S.L. Columbia, 1964

Biophysicist, Columbia, 1958-64
Library Systems Analyst, Columbia, 1964-65
Chief Librarian for Mechanization, Duke University Medical Center, 1965-68
Associate Director, Duke University Medical Center, 1968-

DON L. BOSSEAU, University of Texas, El Paso

B.S. (Engineering) Kansas State University, 1958
M.S. (Engineering) Kansas State University, 1961
M.L.S. University of Hawaii, 1966

Assistant Engineer, GE Aircraft Nuclear Project, Cincinnati, 1957
Engineer, Allis-Chalmers Nuclear Division, Milwaukee, 1958-60
Staff Associate, General Atomic Corporation, La Jolla, 1961-65; Assistant Librarian, 1965
Director, Library Systems Development, University of California, San Diego, 1966-71
Librarian, University of Texas, El Paso
Taught: State University of New York, University of Oregon

GLYN TECWYN EVANS, State University of New York

Chartered Librarian, Liverpool College of Commerce, United Kingdom, 1964

Assistant Librarian, Liverpool Medical Institution, United Kingdom, 1961-64
Librarian, Institute of Neurology, London, United Kingdom, 1964-65
Research Assistant, Royal Society of Medicine, United Kingdom, 1965-68
MEDLARS Liaison Officer, S.E. Region, Royal Society of Medicine, 1967-68
Head, Machine Methods Project, Washington University School of Medicine Library, 1968-71
Acting Deputy Librarian, Washington University School of Medicine Library, 1970-71
Coordinator of Library Systems, Five Associated University Libraries (FAUL), 1971-72
Director of Library Services State University of New York, 1972-

NEIL J. FALVEY, Washington University

    University of Kentucky 1953-54
    Washington University 1954-55
    B.S. (Business Administration) University College, 1965

    Customer Engineer, Electronic Data Processing Division, IBM, 1956-60
    Chief of Computer Operations, U.S. Army Transportation & Mobility Command, 1960-62
    Group Leader, Systems Programming, Monsanto Co., 1962-68
    Group Manager, Data Processing Systems, Washington University, 1968-

VIRGINIA M. FEAGLER, Washington University

    B.A. Indiana University, 1963
    M.S. Indiana University, 1966

    Library Assistant, Biology Library, Indiana University 1963-65
    Serials Assistant, Washington University School of Medicine Library, 1965-68
    Serials Librarian, Washington University School of Medicine Library, 1970-73

JACQUELINE FELTER, Medical Library Center of New York

    B.S. Western Reserve, 1931 (BSLS)

    Branch Librarian, Osterhout Free Library, Wilkes-Barre, Penna., 1931-36
    Librarian, Kingston High School, 1936-42
    Assistant Librarian, then Librarian, New York Post-Graduate Medical School, New York City, 1943-48
    Librarian, Memorial Sloan-Kettering Cancer Center of New York, 1948-49
    Librarian, Medical Society Co., of Queens, New York City, 1960-61

    Director Union Catalog, Medical Library Center of New York, 1961-67
    Acting Director, then Director, Medical Library Center of New York, 1967-

    Associate Editor, Bulletin of Medical Library A., 1957-62. Ed. 1965-66
    Co-Editor, 3rd edition, Handbook of Medical Library Practice, 1969.

MILLARD F. JOHNSON, JR., Washington University

B.S. University of Washington, 1968
M.L.S. University of Washington, 1969
Traineeship in Computer Librarianship, Washington University School of Medicine Library, 1969-70

Systems Analyst, University of Maryland Health Sciences Library, 1970-72
Research Associate, Washington University School of Medicine Library, 1972-

PRISCILLA MAYDEN, University of Utah

B.S. (LS) Simmons, 1941
M.S.L.S. Columbia, 1967

Librarian, Business and Technical Branch, Hartford, Conn. Public Library, 1941-42
Air Base, California, 1945-46
Stewardess, American Air Lines, 1946
Chief Librarian, Veteran's Administration Hospital, Bedford, Mass., 1946-52
Chief Librarian, Veteran's Administration Hospital, Salt Lake City, 1952-66
Medical Sciences Librarian, University of Utah, Salt Lake City, 1966-

President, Utah Library Association, 1961-62

CECILE QUINTAL, National Library of Medicine

M.L.S. in Medical Librarianship, University of Illinois, 1969
National Library of Medicine postgraduate training, 1969-70

Assistant Head, Serial Records & Binding Section, Technical Services Division, National Library of Medicine, 1970-

DEAN A. SCHMIDT, University of Missouri, Columbia

B.A. University of Minnesota, 1951
M.S. (LS), 1953

Junior Librarian, University of Minnesota, 1953-55
U.S. Army, 1955-57
University of Michigan, 1957-62
Medical Librarian, University of Missouri, Columbia, 1962-

PAUL VASSALLO, Library of Congress

B.S. Wayne State University
M.A.L.S. University of Michigan, 1962

Assistant, Wayne State University Law Library, 1959-61
Special Recruit, Library of Congress, 1962-63
Assistant Head, Hispanic Exchange, Section, Library of Congress, 1963
Subject Cataloger, Social Science Division, Library of Congress, 1963-64
Head, Newspaper & Periodical Section, Serials Division, Library of Congress, 1964-65
Assistant Head, Reference Section, Serials Division, Library of Congress, 1965-66
Assistant Chief, Serials Record Division, Library of Congress, 1966-67
Assistant to Dean, Library School, University of Maryland, 1967-68
Chief, Congressional Reference Division, Library of Congress, 1968-71
Chief, National Serials Data Base, 1971-

The Augustan Reprint Society

John Courtenay

A
POETICAL REVIEW
OF THE LITERARY
AND MORAL CHARACTER
OF THE LATE
SAMUEL JOHNSON

(1786)

Introduction by
ROBERT E. KELLEY

PUBLICATION NUMBER 133
WILLIAM ANDREWS CLARK MEMORIAL LIBRARY
UNIVERSITY OF CALIFORNIA, LOS ANGELES
1969